Looking
for Around
GOD

The Oddly Reverent Observations
of an Unconventional Christian

JAMES A. AUTRY

Smyth & Helwys Publishing, Inc.
6316 Peake Road
Macon, Georgia 31210-3960
1-800-747-3016

"Chapter Six: Finding God at Work" has been adapted from James Autry, *Confessions of an Accidental Businessman* (1996). Used by permission of Berrett-Koehler Publishers.

The poem "Messages" was originally published in James Autry, *Confessions of an Accidental Businessman* (1996). Used by permission of Berrett-Koehler Publishers.

The paper used in this publication meets the minimum requirements of
American National Standard for Information Sciences—
Permanence of Paper for Printed Library Materials.
ANSI Z39.48–1984. (alk. paper)

Library of Congress Cataloging-in-Publication Data

Autry, James A.
Looking around for God : The Oddly Reverent
Observations of an Unconventional Christian
by James A. Autry.
p. cm.
ISBN 978-1-57312-484-3 (pbk. : alk. paper)
1. Autry, James A.
2. Christian biography.
3. Christian life–Meditations.
4. Christian life–Poetry.
I. Title.
BR1725.A865A3 2007
277.3'082092–dc22
[B]

2006038949

Advance Praise for
Looking Around for God

In a few deft strokes, in one fell swoop, Jim Autry picks at the most profound presuppositions of belief, tickles the intellect, pricks the conscience, and kicks us all in the seat of the pants.

James M. Dunn
Wake Forest Divinity School

In this wonderful collection of prose and poetry, Jim Autry writes about the spirit and the church with such an unorthodox slant, one wonders if he isn't a prophet. The man's a born poet, maybe even a frustrated preacher. It's a rare gift; an exploration of how much faith there is in doubt and how much grace there is in poetry.

Rev. Patricia DeJong, Senior Minister
First Congregational Church of Berkeley, Ca.

We don't hear the phrase "Christian gentleman" much these days, but that is what James Autry is: generous, large-hearted, tolerant, funny, a man who finds the love of God wherever he can, who pays attention with his heart. Looking Around for God is a book vivid with life and fulfillments. Its honesty is deeply moving, and its irreverence is actually a form of reverence. It's a book that Jesus would have enjoyed.

Stephen Mitchell
Translator of the Tao Te Ching

Dedication

I dedicate this book to the memory of my brother, Ronald, whose own struggles in search of a spiritual path that could honor both his Christian faith and his doubts opened a door for me and set an example I have tried to follow; and also to the memory of my father, a Baptist preacher who was a master of the spoken word.

Contents

Section Two: Looking Unconventionally at the Church

Foreword by Bill Moyers

Yes, it's true: I did urge Jim Autry to write this book. For lesser sins the Good Lord may yet forgive me; this one could be unpardonable. I am now a co-conspirator in the promotion of a heresy that could prove contagious if this book is widely read and Christians snagged in the cul de sac of fundamentalism discover that faith is a continuing and exhilarating course in adult education.

But I accept the hazard of putting in peril my prospects for paradise. We have need of the Gospel According to St. James, and someone had to insist that he put down on paper what privately he had been sharing for so long with a company of old friends and fellow sinners whose eccentric pieties and personal traits and travails have few equals since John Bunyan dined alone at some 17th century English crossroads before beginning his pilgrim's progress. We have sat many an evening around a roaring fire—this band of souls bonded mainly by affection that requires no parsing—as Jim recited a poem he had just written about love and ritual and community, or regaled us from memory with a risqué epic of spiritual exultation taken to carnal extremes, or reported on the latest ground won in the long slow journey to independent living of the autistic son he and Sally have loved and esteemed since birth.

And on each of these occasions I have marveled at the faith of a man who had said he had little. Not that he had put it quite that way. But there was no doubt among those of us who knew him that some where back there he had taken down the theses his father and grandfather had nailed to the door of the Baptist church in Pine Grove, Mississippi. It was less a revolt against what he had been taught than it was a revelation, not uncommon to Fundamentalist progeny, that the world was far more complicated, and faith far more confounding, than had been taught in Vacation Bible School or during "sword drills" of Biblical texts that were a fixture of the boot camp indoctrination of a Baptist Training Union. Jim didn't really go AWOL; he simply decided not to fight a phony war.

The first time I heard him read a poem, however, I recognized a voice resonant with the values and verities of a faith achieved not by rote recitation of creed or confession but from wrestling, like Jacob, with unnamed and unexpected visitations, with life itself, and with the desperate choices we must often make in the dark, alone, groping for balance and sanity and hope, without a single candle's glow. The Christ who shows up there, if at all, looks nothing like the wan Jesus of the Sunday School poster; this Christ arrives – unexpected, uninvited, invisible – simply as Presence.

The fellow reading that poem as the fire crackled in the Vermont chill had experienced such moments; of this I was certain. At the time he was president of the magazine group of the Meredith Corporation, a Fortune 500 media giant among whose publications was Better Homes and Gardens, with the fourth-largest circulation in the world. His day began with profit margins and ended with the bottom line and in between came hard decisions about incompetent or redundant employees. The subject of Jim's poem this night was "Thoughts on Firing a Salesman:"

"It's like a little murder,
  taking his life,
  his reason for getting on the train...."

"A murder with no funeral," he read on, and everyone in that room realized the poet himself had signed the pink slip and never forgotten the wounding he had inflicted. He knows about suffering, I thought, and the unintended consequences we visit upon others. This was not a sensibility fashioned in business school, and I wanted to know more about its source. The next day I spent the afternoon reading Jim's first book of poetry, *Nights Under a Tin Roof*, encountering in it the people and sounds and sights of rural Mississippi and the congregations to which his forebears had ministered and the kinfolk among whom he had been succored. Oh, my, I said to myself – I knew these people: Aunt Cassie, Cousins Lester, Lottie and Callie, Brother Jim Goff, the McIlhenneys. I knew "about babies born and people cured/about fires and broken bones and cows loose and dogs lost" from my own days in Oklahoma's Little Dixie and the piney woods of East Texas, and among the peanut farmers and cotton growers and roughnecks at churches in Loco, Shiloh, Brandon, and Weir. I knew that you can no more get these people out of your heart than you can wash the red clay and black clods from between your toes with a single scrubbing.

At the time I was working on a PBS series about poetry and I asked Jim to take me down to Pine Grove where we could film some of his people and talk about language, faith, and life. We stopped at the county store where Cousin Ira McGaughey spoke of "Erse" – as in "Erse is doing this" instead of "we" – and visited people who referred to "chirren" instead of children and heard a lady in the church kitchen explaining the tardiness of a companion with a simple, "I don't know. She's just a'blowin' and a'goin'." Sitting under a gnarled tree on the church grounds, with the cameras running, we talked about how language and religion here caught life on the run and how both were made to fit the way things were in a place without illusions. Jim's father had pastored the church 33 years, stalking the congregation with fire and brimstone and powerful stories while mopping his face with a red bandanna, and Jim still heard his father's voice in his head, still saw in his mind's eye the red sweaty handkerchief. You will meet the elder Autry later in these pages and after you read "Prayer for a Country Preacher"

> ….preaching a revival meeting
>   with the congregation eager beyond discomfort
>   on a wet and insect laden night

> …singing bass
>   on a Sunday morning
>   his head above the others
>   his voice bringing power beyond
>   power in the blood

...praying
at a table of summer Sunday food
fried chicken and sliced tomatoes
and peas and cornbread and tea
with his family around him
like disciples

you will not forget him, either.

There were, of course, dark stains in those woods, bad things done by Jesus-loving people, and Jim said to me on camera that he had spent a lot of his life trying not to be a white Southerner. I was sure this had figured in his turning away from the Old Story. But he sprang from the loins of a powerful faith; it is in his DNA. Over a long life of joy and sadness, triumphs and troubles, wins and losses, he has held that faith up to the light, examined its assumptions, recognized its pretentions, shed its superstitions, tested it against experience, and, like a man pouring new wine into an old bottle, settled on what is vibrant and valuable. Well, not exactly settled; this is a man for whom faith is a deep flowing current that carries him from one shore to another, and, sometimes, home again, even when home turns out to be a place unexpected. That is the mystery of it. The road to truth often runs through the byways of heresy. That is the power of it.

For years now he and I have talked about all this, and he has finally obliged my repeated requests to write an account of his faith journey. There is much to be savored here, and much to learn. I'll wager you don't know why Jesus really threw the money changers out of the Temple, or why the Parable of the Good Samaritan smacked the religious big boys where it hurts, or why there was no room in the inn for the 14-year-old Mary, pregnant with Jesus. There is, by the way, sex in this book. And prayer. And poetry. Such poetry!

My friend writes as if he is engaged in an intimate conversation. That is why I urged him to write this book – to draw you into the circle too. So,

Father, forgive me.
I knew what I was doing
And did it anyway.
Because, Lord, there is good news in this book
For those with eyes to see and ears to hear.

Acknowledgments

Several years ago at a gathering of friends, Bill Moyers said to me, "You should write a book and call it *Becoming a Christian Again for the First Time*." It took a few minutes for me to realize he was serious. I think he was reacting to some of the poetry I'd shared with the group as well as to our conversations about how we had both moved from fairly hard-shell Southern Baptist backgrounds to what would probably be described as progressive mainline Protestantism. Bill knew it had been a difficult journey for me.

I must also acknowledge the Gulley Group—they know who they are—in whose presence I have been blessed and led along a path made richer and more intense. There are no words to describe the love, respect, and appreciation I have for these friends.

This book probably would have stayed in my computer forever had it not been for my friend, James Dunn, who encouraged me to send the manuscript to Mark McElroy and Keith Gammons at Smyth & Helwys. Thank you, James.

Along the way, I have shared these essays and poems with friends whose eyes and ears I trust implicitly. At the top of that list was the late Michelle Urry, who took an almost proprietary interest in this work and who brought a light into my day when I needed it.

I include also my dear friend Betty Sue Flowers, who has read, critiqued, encouraged, and supported me not only in this book but in almost everything I've written for twenty-six years.

A very important person in expanding my "Christian education" is Rev. Ms. Pat DeJong, who also encouraged me for years to publish this collection.

I don't know how other authors work, but with me, writing a book is definitely not a one-person endeavor. I have no shame when it comes to leaning on my friends.

Finally, as always, I owe my wife, Sally Pederson, the credit for keeping me sane and balanced.

—James A. Autry

Author's Note: There are new and selected poems throughout this book. Previously published poems have been so noted. All of these poems are mine with the exception of two, one by my wife Sally and the other by my son Jimmy.

Preface

"His eye is on the sparrow, and I know he watches me."

The message of this old spiritual, sung by thousands of gospel choirs and soloists, probably is most often interpreted as one of comfort and reassurance that God is watching over each of us individually. Certainly that interpretation helped my mother through her years of pain and challenge as a single parent.

But the message came to me with quite a different meaning. In the fundamentalist church of my youth, it was yet another warning that I had better behave in a Christian way, because if God could keep an eye on every sparrow, He could surely keep an eye on me and would know when I did anything sinful. The idea of an all-knowing and all-seeing God became a heavy burden.

I admit that I gave up on Christianity for a long time. I figured we all might be better off if we just gave Jesus a rest for a while. The more I saw of some Christians and how they seemed to want to recreate our world in an image I would not be able to recognize as "Christian," the more I thought, *Why encourage them by even participating?*

At the same time, I realized deep within me that I was a Christian, but it had not been a smooth path. Even as a high school student, I found myself growing more and more skeptical of religion as I was experiencing it as a young person in the Protestant South, so when I finally went off to college I stopped going to church altogether. Yes, I felt guilty from time to time, and when I shuttled back and forth between the homes of my divorced parents, I went to church with them. My father was a Southern Baptist minister, and when I visited him, I was even asked occasionally to lead the congregational singing. But if those churches hadn't included among the congregants a supply of dateable girls, I'd have been a lot less interested in worship.

In those days, I never heard the phrase "spiritual journey." While many college students at that time must have studied matters of religion and philosophy, I in my journalism/English education did not get any of that—and I can assure you that religion and the inner life were not part of our late-night dormitory discussions.

In the 1970s, when I was in my late forties, I found myself associating with people who had an entirely different orientation to religion and to spirituality. When introduced to Jung and the idea of a universal unconscious, I was astounded, as I was later when reading about synchronicity. Fritjof Capra's and Gary Zukav's writings about the mysteries of quantum mechanics delighted and fascinated me on the one hand, and emphasized how ignorant I was on the other. But that ignorance became a quest to learn more about the mysteries of the world, mysteries that seemed to me connected to a power beyond anything we could define or identify, except perhaps as the great unknown, the higher power, the ultimate reality, God. Yet at that time, I did not feel the church would offer me the opportunity to learn and grow as I wanted.

Friends became my teachers and let me hitchhike on their spiritual journeys, and those kindnesses helped me get closer to my own path. I went to weekend spiritual retreats of various kinds, associated mostly with the human potential movement or what some people like to call "New Age" philosophy (although I've never been able to define that term.)

I have fundamentalist Christian friends and family who seem threatened by the "New Age," its focus on connectedness, and its openness to Eastern philosophy and religion, but to the contrary it was through these experiences that I found my way back to my Christian faith. I had worked hard to learn to meditate, without much success, but finally I came back to prayer. However, it was a different kind of prayer: not prayers focused on my laundry list of what I want God to give me, but prayers focused on others.

The story of a fundamentalist-reared Christian rebelling against his upbringing and then finding his way back to religion is an old story, and I won't beat it to death again on these pages. But fast-forwarding through and looking back at the years—marriage, children, divorce, remarriage, careers, and success, with traditional church-going as well as experimentation with other religions and spiritual disciplines interspersed throughout—I realize that I have experienced the presence of the divine many times, and still seek to experience it many more times. Some people refer to that as a spiritual quest. I call it "looking around for God."

I think it's important to keep on looking because I believe God is partly in the looking itself. Besides, I never know where I might just happen upon God, perhaps someplace I've looked a thousand times but never noticed God was there. I could even say God sneaks up on us, but the fact is that God is always there; we just have trouble seeing God, not because we keep looking in all the wrong places—there are no wrong places—but because we are looking at the wrong angle or we are wearing the filter of our expectations. We expect to find God in a certain place or in a certain way; we expect signs from the heavens; we expect to find God where we want God to be.

In fact, I'm sure that experiencing the divine depends on each person's life circumstances or background or interests. The nature lover, the musician, the poet, the scholar, the athlete may more readily find God within those experiences. Mies van der Rohe once said about architecture that "God is in the details."

Having spent my life as a generalist, I don't think I had a particular filter of expectation, and perhaps that's why I began to see God popping up here and there. At first I didn't recognize what was happening, but I knew something had happened. I felt touched, visited, even transformed in my thinking.

From those unexpected and surprising times that I felt "with" God, I began to open myself to the possibilities that God was all around me and that I would do well to be attentive. This is probably another way of saying I wanted to remain open to the presence, or the possibilities, of God. I realize, even in saying this, that I risk sounding phony, like some otherworldly spiritual seeker who, having now found God, is passionate to share the inner journey with others, to show the way, to witness.

Nothing of the sort. I don't fancy myself a guru, prophet, or even a seeker for that matter. I'm a writer and poet, a former jet fighter pilot, editor, and business executive. I claim no theological credentials, no enlightenment or road-to-Damascus conversion experience, no spiritual insights, no nothing. I claim only to have found that, although my Christianity may be unconventional, I nonetheless profess it because those values are deeply part of my consciousness. I can accept the community and ritual and liturgy of the church and I can participate fully in it without being controlled by the institution of it; I can accept and respect and learn from the truths of other faiths because I realize that no religion has the only truth; and most important, I can find God if only I pay attention to everything and everyone around me.

I think the true message of that old spiritual is not just that God has an eye on the sparrow. It's that God is demonstrating that if these details are worth God's attention, they are certainly worth ours. It may be that we will more readily find God in the details of this world, and of our own lives, than anywhere else.

In assembling these personal essays and stories and poems, I have had two goals. One was to share how God has been revealed in many different circumstances of my life. I've not attempted to be explicit about that in every instance, hoping it will be self-evident. My second goal was to draw on the experiences of my own journey to comment on the Christian churches of my experience and offer a few ideas for how they might better serve in making God's love and presence manifest in the world.

Some of you may find here irreverence—perhaps even heresy—but I fervently believe that these writings are, at their heart, deeply reverent.

My greatest hope is that these words will be helpful to you and perhaps will stimulate you to begin your own journey. If you've read this far, you may already have begun.

Section One:

Looking Around for God Every Day

Chapter One

Lessons from the Heart

Friends told me that heart surgery would change the rest of my life. And they didn't mean diet and exercise. I was told I would become more spiritual; some people said I'd find myself more involved in religion and religious activities, that my whole view of the world would change.

In other words, the doctors would stop my heart, reroute some arteries, and restart a man more aware of his mortality and more inspired to see himself on the path to heaven in the time between the trial run at death and the real thing.

I didn't pay much attention to those friends. My main reaction to the surgery was that it was a massive inconvenience, and while I appreciated intensely the skill of the doctors and nurses, plus the technology involved, I confess that I thought of the whole process as a sophisticated plumbing repair job.

I don't mean to sound cavalier; I was plenty worried. But my focus was on getting through the ordeal and returning to a life that was already balanced, grounded, and happy, a life of loving family and friends, of meaningful and worthwhile work, of seemingly boundless opportunity, despite my being in my sixties. So after those five miserable days in the hospital, I returned home with truly no thought of having been at death's door or of having been somehow changed.

But something happened. It's difficult to explain or even describe, but I found myself enveloped by mysterious sensations. First, the setting: I could not climb stairs to my home office and could do little physical activity beyond walking for the prescribed number of minutes each day and breathing into a device intended to keep my lungs clear and strong. A good friend brought over a big reclining chair that I surrounded with a phone, a computer, and a stack of get-well wishes I intended to answer. So I was organized, as comfortable as possible for my condition, and determined to get on with life. No change in my worldview.

But when I awoke from a nap on that first day at home, I found the world around me transformed. I scribbled these notes: "The afternoon light is slanting into the room, catching the many flowers friends have sent, and intensifying the colors. The light, the flowers, the fabric on the furniture, all of it glows. There's no other word. It's almost eerie; I've looked across this room a thousand times and never seen this glow, as if I can feel it or even breathe it, like the interchange of senses I've read about in which blind people 'see' colors by touching them. I'm suddenly feeling so grateful. If the doctors had to cut me open for this, it was worth it."

I know this sounds like the mutterings from a drug-induced psychedelic episode out of the 1960s or '70s. There are those younger than I who no doubt will nod knowingly at my descriptions of the light and color and think, "Been there, done that." If indeed they have been there and done that, all I can say is I hope they haven't forgotten the experience or the message.

Other people might offer the scientific explanation that I was still withdrawing from the anesthesia and was mildly hallucinating. Whatever reaction or explanation others may have, I can only respond that I don't care. I care only that I was filled with gratitude. Not just for my life but for the light, the flowers, the colors, the room, the glow itself. I wrote, "I understand more fully now what Meister Eckhardt meant when he said, 'When praying, it is enough to say thank you.'"

A similar phenomenon occurred the next day when Beethoven's Sixth Symphony came on my sound system. From my notes: "The music, like yesterday's light, is richer, more intense, more complex than anything I've heard. Could this have been what Beethoven himself was hearing? Would he be happy that, across the centuries, he has made this connection with me, a middle-class man in a city in a world he never heard of? I hope so. There is a story that Beethoven, after losing his hearing, had the legs cut down on his piano so he could 'hear' the vibrations and feel the music through his body. Genius out of disability. And I can feel this music in my body, more than just through my ears, as if I am absorbing it somehow and, in doing so, becoming almost part of it or vice-versa."

Again, I realize these kinds of experiences may yield to one explanation or another. But they were revelatory to me because I felt connected with something much greater than myself, with the music and with the light as forces beyond how we usually identify them—as, I might say, manifestations of God.

The revelations did not end during the next few weeks, though they were less dramatic. As I sat in the recliner day after day, forced to be still and observe and think, rather than be up and doing and reacting, everything seemed more intense. The experience recalled all the largely ignored admonitions from poets as well as prophets to "be still," to "keep silent."

As I write this, I understand the futility of trying to describe the indescribable, and I feel the frustration of knowing that the more I write the more I risk trivializing the experience.

So heart surgery did not scare me into repentance. But coming face to face with my own mortality lifted the veil, made vivid the sacred hues and notes that had surrounded me unnoticed for years.

As for repentance, I'm not sure we should spend all that much time on repentance anyway. A lot of people seem preoccupied with their sins and their need for repentance, but I think we should just admit the failings, accept the forgiveness that's already there, and be done with it. Then move on to the next logical step: gratitude. Live in gratitude. That is the lesson from my heart.

Sunrise Flight into Chicago

Who can say this is not beautiful,
lake, skyline, street lights,
traffic beginning to move,
even with every mean thing
going on down there,
the muggings, the accidents, the layoffs,

the infidelities and betrayals
stretching from the tenements to the suburbs?
With all of that it still gathers its energy
for another start,
it still dawns a new day,
perhaps even the better day we all hope for.

Chapter Two

God at the Track Meet

In the past several years, fundamentalist TV ministers and others have expressed great angst about how "they've kicked God out of the schools." These critics then describe our school systems as overstaffed and wasteful; our teachers as unresponsive and ineffective; our students as self-absorbed slackers.

I'm tired of hearing it, but my intention here is not to debate. Rather, I, as one parent of one student in one school, want to tell you a story about a track meet.

Five years ago, our son, Ronald was a freshman at Roosevelt High School in Des Moines, Iowa. He has autism. When he was three, he still could not walk well. His motor skills were deficient and he had not learned the simple reflex of putting up his hands when he fell, so even on the simplest walks in the neighborhood, Ronald would fall on his forehead. He had a large red knot there for months at a time. I would have helped him more, held his hand, protected him, but my wife Sally, God bless her, insisted that we encourage him to make it by himself even if it meant falling.

Even though he's still not the most coordinated young man in town, he joined the Roosevelt marching band, then in the spring he went out for track. Once again, I credit Sally for being the risk-taker. It hurts me so much to see him in embarrassing situations that I'd probably overprotect him, but she is more concerned with making a good effort than with embarrassment.

The track coach welcomed him to the team and told him he'd run the 400 meter and occasionally the 200 meter. I will never forget the first track meet in which he was to run the 400.

It was a cool day, so the team members wore sweat suits over their "silks." Immediately, this concerned me because it meant Ronald would have to take off his sweat pants in order to run, which also meant he'd have to take off his shoes and put them on again.

At the time, Ronald still occasionally put his shoes on the wrong feet. So I was worried about the possible embarrassment of that. He also still tied his shoes the way he did when he first learned to do it. One of the characteristics of his autism is that once he learns how to do something, he does it that way every time. The shoes were likely to come untied during the run.

Sure enough, when it was time to get ready, Ronald took off his shoes and put them back on the wrong feet. I was watching this through the lens of a camcorder because I promised I'd tape his run. I was too far away to call to him, but one of his teammates knelt close to him and discreetly pointed out the shoe situation; Ronald changed them.

He went to the starting line. I kept thinking to myself, *Is it wrong to put him through this? Will he just be embarrassed? What does this prove?*

The gun sounded and Ronald began. He fell immediately behind, but that was okay because I knew his objective was to run the full 400 without stopping or falling. He fell farther and farther behind; his shoes came untied, but he kept going. When the other participants crossed the finish line, Ronald was only about halfway around.

I kept the camcorder on him. As he came around the last turn toward the finish, I caught in the corner of my eye some of his teammates in the infield. They had started running with him and were calling to him, "Go Ronald! Go Ronald!"

As Ronald came closer to the bleachers, other people began to take up the cry. "Go Ronald!" And as he passed in front of the crowd, the cry swept across the stands; parents of other kids from other schools had picked up his name and were yelling, "Go Ronald!"

Ronald smiled and ran. When he crossed the finish line, the crowd was roaring as if an Olympic star had just set a new record. To my ears it was like the sounds of the heavenly host, rejoicing. By then, of course, my camcorder viewfinder was blurred with tears, but I did see members of other teams high-five Ronald after the race, pat him on the back, shout words of encouragement. I didn't see any "self-involved slackers," only decent, sensitive, and supportive young men and women.

I realized then that Ronald's run was not about me or my worries of embarrassment; it was about him and those other young people and those other parents, and somehow also about how Ronald had given them the chance to reveal the divine within themselves.

Later, I asked Ronald, "What were you thinking as you ran?" He said, "You can do it, Ronald, you can do it." Indeed he did.

Thirty years ago, he might not have had the option of a somewhat normal high school experience. Yet he spent four years in the midst of a thriving, diverse, supportive public high school. He's eccentric, yes. He can be difficult, yes. And he sure won't set any speed records. But, by the grace of God and an enlightened public education system, *Ronald is in the race.*

Egypt (3/31/90)

We stopped at the Cairo Carpet School,
a dozen ladies looking for a bargain.
Unsuspecting.
The schoolmaster spoke with pride,
"The children come to us at five or six years old.
We like to get them young so they can
learn the trade quickly.
They work for four hours with a break after two.
And we give them a free meal every day."
He smiled.

They sit there in a row
on low benches in front of the looms,
tying colored threads to match the paper
pattern hanging before them.
Their tiny fingers move deftly, machine-like,

over, under, looping and
knotting the silk string.
There's a lump in my throat.
Upstairs in the showroom we see
the magic silk carpets change colors
before our eyes
when the salesman turns them
side to side.
"Handmade. Very good price."

But standing downstairs, among the children
I cannot help but think of my six-year-old
who cannot tie his shoes
and would not be so lucky
as these children
if his soul had been born
to an Egyptian child.

—*Sally Pederson*

Chapter Three

Finding Life's Lessons in the Death Notices

Don't ask why because I don't know, but lately I've been reading the obituaries. Not the ones with large headlines about the passing of some publicly notable person, but the small ones with a tiny photograph and three or four short paragraphs.

Usually there is one sentence describing accomplishments and another describing interests. I often find myself moved emotionally by what is contained in those two sentences, the modest record of lives well lived, of service to fellow human beings, of contributions as vital to the well-being of community and country as anything described in the obituaries with the big headlines. What always strikes me most is the pride in work or a job, in volunteer and church activities, in sports or hobbies or military service.

I suppose a social scientist might observe nothing extraordinary in these little stories, but after reading hundreds of them, I have the impression of a complex mosaic of acts large and small that together create the spiritual ebb and flow of a community. I get the feeling that I knew these people, that they were my people. They had families, did their work, and did their duty, some by answering the call of country and others by answering the needs of the less fortunate. I find a richness of spirit and feel the presence of the sacred in the everydayness of their lives.

I have a large collection of these stories, but here are a few excerpts. Read them and see for yourself what I mean:

- "He was a retired salesman with Electrolux Corp. and a member of St. John's Catholic Church and Coal Miners Association. He played the accordion for several years at care centers."
- "He was a volunteer with Generations and annually spoke to kindergarten students at St. Augustine's Catholic School about his life as a disabled person. He was an avid John Wayne fan."
- "She was a member of Heartland Senior Services and Alcoholics Anonymous."
- "She was a member of God's Family Church and enjoyed volunteering, taking walks with her granddaughter and finding feathers."
- "He enjoyed repairing small engines."
- "She was a retired housekeeper for Howard Johnson's Motel. She enjoyed flowers and boat rides."
- "He was the lead man in the mix room at Meadow Gold-Beatrice Foods before retiring."
- "He was a member of the Adel Fire Department. He enjoyed public speaking, interpretive readings, and oratory presentations."
- "She was a member of Capitol Hill Christian Church and Des Moines Area Quilters Guild and was well known for making quilts."
- "She had been a bookkeeper at Ace Cab in Las Vegas and enjoyed sewing."
- "He was a member of the Iowa Softball Hall of Fame and Veterans of Foreign Wars. He was proud of bowling a perfect game in November 1982."
- "She was crowned Plowman's Queen in 1948 by President Harry Truman at the National Plowing contest."
- "She had traveled across Iowa giving ballroom dancing lessons."
- "He was an avid gardener and enjoyed raising miniature donkeys."
- "She had been a waitress at Bankers Life Cafeteria."
- "He was devoted to the Fire Department and its staff."
- "She was a 'Rosie the Riveter' welder in the shipyards during World War II."
- "He had a passion for buying and restoring antique furniture."
- "She enjoyed reading the Bible."
- "She had been a clerk for various businesses . . . and had cared for her aged parents and sisters."

- "She was an accomplished seamstress whose creations have been worn at several weddings and special events."
- "Farming was his life."
- "She was a member of Central United Methodist Church . . . and had helped many people in caring for their loved ones."

There are two lessons I take from all these stories: One is that the way God's love is made manifest in the world is through our everyday acts of service and caring. The other is that there are no small accomplishments, no small contributions, no unimportant jobs. And there are no "ordinary" people; every life can make a difference for some other life and thus make a difference in the world. It is not what we choose to do so much as how we set ourselves to do it—our commitment, our pride, our belief in work well done and responsibilities well met—that makes our lives matter.

Meditation

All I really know about life I can say
in a few lines:
In April the small green things
rise through the black Iowa soil
whether we're ready or not.
The Carolina wren makes her nest
in the little redwood house
my son built from a kit.
Daffodils, tulips, Irises get the attention as usual
while purslane, pig weed, and lamb's quarters
quietly take over a place
while no one is watching.

In June the corn shoots
etch long green lines
across the dark loamy fields,
and the greenest of all green grasses

crowd into the ditches and line the roads.
In August the early bloomers
begin to burn themselves out,
but in September the late yellows appear,
luring the bumblebees and yellowjackets
into a frenzy of pollination.

You already know about October,
the color, the last burst of extravagant life.
And then all at once it seems
everything retreats, pulls into itself, rests,
and prepares for the inevitable resurrection.

Chapter Four

Simple Gifts

I recently attended the funeral of a friend, a man who had suffered for about eighteen months with a debilitating and crippling disease. It struck me, as it always does, that there is so little we can do, so little we can say, at those sad times.

Yet in the weeks leading up to his death and in the weeks afterward, his friends tried to do all they could do and say all they could say. One day I visited him at the hospice. He sat in a wheel chair, his body shockingly emaciated but his eyes still bright and aware. In front of him on a table were cheeses, breads, and wine. A steady stream of friends came and went; my friend greeted them with his eyes and even used an alphabet board to communicate words.

All of us told stories in which our friend was the principal character. There was much laughter. We hugged him and one another; we tried to reassure his wife and other family members that we'd be there to help; we tried to reassure one another that we'd be okay without him.

With the wine and the cheese and the stories and the reassurances, we were bringing what we could, our gifts. Simple gifts, yes, but our gifts nonetheless.

Maybe that's what we're supposed to give when there's nothing else to give.

My wife recently told me a story about Chan Pen, an Asian American woman whose profession is manicurist, and one of her long-time weekly customers who became severely disabled several years ago. This woman had always been fastidious about her fingernails, and when her illness deprived her of mobility, her husband continued to bring her in a wheelchair every week so Chan Pen could do her nails.

Then one week she did not show up; the husband called to say she'd died. Chan Pen offered to do her nails one last time, this time for the funeral. I have this mental image of Chan Pen working diligently to make this final manicure the best she'd ever done. At no charge, of course. A simple gift.

I recall the warm spring day of my mother's funeral in Blue Mountain, Mississippi. I decided to visit the cemetery a few hours before the service. There I found an African American man digging my mother's grave with a shovel. Digging a grave by hand in that red Mississippi soil is unbelievably hard work, and I wondered why he was doing it that way.

I introduced myself. We talked a few minutes, and I said I thought graves were dug by machine these days. He made it clear that he wanted to dig this particular grave by hand. You see, as a grave digger, this was all he could do, his simple gift to my mother, a woman who had befriended him and treated him with kindness and dignity.

I want to believe we are able to connect spiritually in times of great joy and celebration, and I'm sure that's true to some extent, but in my experience, those connections seem easier and more natural in times of sadness and loss. As for the simple gifts, they are but the expressions of that spiritual connection, offerings of ourselves that we lay on the altar of our common humanity and love.

Grave Digger

His name is Otis Cox
and the graves he digs with a spade are acts of love.

The red clay holds like concrete
still he makes it give up a place
for rich caskets and poor
working with sweat and sand
in the springing tightness of his hair
saying that machine digging

don't seem right if you know
the dead person.

His pauses are slow as the digging
a foot always on the shovel.
Shaking a sad and wet face
drying his sorrow with a dust orange white handkerchief
he delivers a eulogy
"Miz Ruth always gimme a dlipper of water."

Then among quail calls and Blackeyed Susans
Otis Cox shapes with grunt and sweat and shovel
a perfect work
a mystical place
a last connection with the living hand.

—From *Nights Under a Tin Roof*, 1983

Chapter Five

Embracing the Everyday Holiness

What makes things or places sacred? I've wondered about this over the years. I remember visiting some of the great cathedrals of Europe not long after World War II when I was stationed in France with the Air Force. I was not very religious in those days and, as a Southern Baptist in my youth, never had a high regard for the Catholic Church generally, so I visited churches only as tourist attractions.

But I remember how suddenly quiet and reverent I felt as soon as I entered those mighty, cavernous spaces. I felt the same way regardless of the church or the country. Many years later, when my wife and I traveled to Europe, we stopped at every church we passed, most of them Catholic, and lit a candle for our remembered family and for our son Ronald (a practice completely foreign to our own Protestant experiences), and we prayed silently. I felt always I was in a sacred place.

But why? Was it that the place was a church? Or that worship services were celebrated there? Or that the structure had somehow been sanctified through a ritual of the church?

No, I think it was simply because so many people had come to the place over so many years, bringing with them the expectation that they were entering a sacred place. In other words, in their quest and in their expectations of a connection with God, *the people created the sacred space within the building*, a space that was so palpable I could feel it when I entered—even though I personally held no such expectation of the connection with God.

How do I explain that further? I don't. I just accept it, and in that acceptance I've also come to realize that it is not just in houses of worship that I should seek the presence of the sacred, but in everything I do and experience, even the mundane stuff.

I've read that Hasidic Jews find the holy in the everyday, whether washing the dishes, eating a meal, or making love. I admire this attitude, and if what I believe is true, that the consciousness of a connection with God in effect creates the holiness we feel in a church, then why would this not be true anywhere?

In the past few years, I've come to understand and embrace these possibilities more fully. In 1998, the winner of the Democratic gubernatorial primary in our state asked my wife, Sally Pederson, to be his running mate. Though she had never sought political office before, she is now in her second term as lieutenant governor of Iowa.

The whole thing—the campaign and the subsequent life as a public servant—has been a shock. Neither Sally nor I had the slightest notion of what the public expects of its elected officials. To get past this part of the story quickly, the answer is "a lot." Sally is busy almost every day, seven days a week, with few days off.

From the day of her nomination, I have taken responsibility for all housework and childcare, all budgeting and bill paying, all doctor, dentist, and veterinary appointments, all automobile maintenance, all lawn and garden work, and all grocery shopping and cooking. This is in addition to my profession as author, consultant, and speaker.

It is a cliché, I know, but it is true that every working spouse and parent should give the stay-at-home role a try. The demands are incessant, the requirement for attention to detail rivals any detail-oriented job on earth, and the responsibilities for other lives far outweighs that of any business manager.

Beyond the intellectual realization that, in taking over this role and supporting my wife and son, I am doing important work, I also derive great emotional fulfillment from it, and in ways I would never have suspected.

One way is in the simple satisfaction I feel after cooking a good meal or cleaning the kitchen. I like the way my son's clothes smell when they come out of the dryer, and it gives me a sense of accomplishment when I put them into his dresser, ready for the next week of school.

I confess I get a kick out of defying the stereotype of the clueless husband. Recently, I went to lunch with an old friend. When she dug down into her purse, a panty liner fell out onto the floor. She didn't notice. I retrieved it, handed it to her, and said, "Here's your panty liner."

"What did you say?" she asked in a tone of surprise, almost astonishment.

"I said, 'Here's your panty liner.'"

She laughed and shook her head. "My husband wouldn't have the slightest idea what a panty liner is."

Enjoying myself immensely, I responded, "I can even tell you brands and types, light days or heavy days, scented or unscented." By this time she was laughing.

"I buy these things for Sally," I said. "She doesn't have time to pick them up, and I can't imagine her asking her security trooper to stop by the store so she can run in for some panty liners."

"And you aren't embarrassed?" my friend asked.

"Of course not. Why should I be embarrassed about panty liners and not about toilet paper or hemorrhoid cream or something like that? This is just human stuff."

But while defying the stereotypes is fun, and while I know the household work is important, there is more to it, something beyond emotional fulfillment, something deeper, something about meaning and connection with everyday holiness, something spiritual.

I think my desire to seek God in the details of everyday life has a lot to do with facing and evaluating how I used to live. For years, I made lists of chores for the weekends, and as I did them I dutifully checked them off the list. There was a certain satisfaction in getting through the list, but the psychological pitfall was that if I did not complete a chore and check it off, it was as if I'd done nothing. It was almost like a failure.

I'd read a lot of the stuff about how the journey is the destination and how growing spiritually is in the very process of spiritual growth, but I had managed to put that in some kind of compartment, as if spiritual growth was part of the list of things to do, stuck somewhere in there with cleaning the gutters and mowing the lawn: "Okay, I've grown spiritually, now where's the hedge trimmer?"

It took a while but I finally got it: What I'd read was not about adding a spiritual growth compartment to my life but trying to live all my life with the daily consciousness of a potential for holiness in everything and with the realization that everything I do is part of something larger.

I realized that my spiritual journey, my connection with the sacred, could include such unlikely things as cleaning the gutters, mowing the lawn, trimming the hedge, changing diapers, doing the laundry, cooking meals, and even buying panty liners for my wife. Of course, it's easier in some places and with some activities than with others. For instance, working in my greenhouse or garden will always give me a holiness fix when I need it. Still, it's possible anywhere.

Am I successful every day? Of course not. I still become impatient and frustrated. I still give in to just getting through the list and checking things off. But at least I am aware of when I'm falling short of my intentions, and I have come to believe that awareness of those failings may even be more important in the longer journey. As the Zen master said, "Everything is perfect but there's still room for improvement."

The Resurrection
—For Jim Gilliom, Easter Sunday, 1994

This story is about a little girl
who died on Easter Sunday
and about her father who could no longer whistle.
Everyone knew at once,
the family, the neighbors,
that life would never be the same
without the little girl,
but it took a while for everyone to realize
that life would never be the same
without the father's whistle.

No one tried to talk him into it
because they understood the whistle
was somehow with the little girl,
gone, it seemed, forever.

Nobody knew what happened that day at the plant,
or if anything did,
but even before he arrived home
a neighbor lady called to say
how much it meant to hear the whistle.
"Your father has started whistling again,"
the mother told her son,
who then carried the father's tune in his heart
until one Easter Sunday
many years later and many miles away,
in a sermon of resurrection,
the son was able at last to tell this story,
and to whistle.

And the spirit of his father was released
as a blessing to all who heard it.

Chapter Six

Finding God at Work

We may not be, as some suggest, "called" to work. We may indeed start working to make money, to improve our status, to create a future, or just to stay off the dole, as they used to say.

I was reluctant to get a job when I was a kid. I did not want to work. It seemed inconvenient, far too wasteful of my time. But we were poor. I did a little of everything—carried the morning newspaper on a regular route, then later in the day sold the afternoon paper to businessmen who would stop by my corner on the way home from the office; chopped cotton and picked cotton on a farm; worked on a bread truck, on a construction crew, and as a soda jerk, waiter, copy boy, photographer's assistant, teletype operator, musician, reporter, and photographer—before I graduated from college. And this does not include my work scholarships as a university public relations writer, darkroom technician, and—yes, I got paid to do it—drum major of the university marching band.

Not one of those jobs did I do for anything but money. Not for training or education, not for the advancement of a career, not to create a productive future, and certainly not for personal or spiritual growth. Only for money.

My mother worked in degrading low-level jobs only because she had to make money. I recall how proud she was when she was given some training on a "comptometer machine," which I surmised was some kind of calculator. I realize now that the reason learning to operate that machine meant so much to her was because it evidenced a skill, the mastery of something almost mystical that elevated her to another plane of achievement, in her mind something like a professional.

And of course, she credited God. She felt God had, as in the old hymn, planted her feet on higher ground. Her belief that God had helped her did not stop there. God had helped her for a reason, and the reason was that she would now be in a better position to "witness for Jesus." This, in her view, was what we all were to do, those of us who called ourselves Christians.

"Jimmy," she would tell me, "you surely can use your paper route to witness for Jesus." Naturally I thought that to be impossible. What was I supposed to do, ask one of the people in the mansions I serviced at one end of my route or someone in the poor white shotgun houses at the other end of the route, "Have you accepted Jesus as your personal savior?" or "Would you like to go to church with me?" I remember once or twice trying to summon the courage to approach the subject with one of my customers, but I did not have Mother's confidence that the Lord would save me from ridicule and embarrassment.

That is still my fear as I speak and write about the spirit of work. Still, I know that the liberation of the human spirit in the context of the work we choose to do—even if we choose that work only for the money—is at the heart of the healing that must happen if we are to save American business from a debilitating and destructive crisis of trust in the wake of the reengineering and downsizing and outsourcing of the past several years.

No, it's not the same as witnessing for Jesus, yet I do believe our daily work gives us the best opportunities to look for the best—the divine—in others and to manifest the best—the divine—in ourselves. Indeed, I believe any good work we do for or with others is also God's work.

Just what is good work with others? It's any work, no matter how routine or menial, done with generosity, positive intention, a spirit of community, and a commitment to doing it well.

What is good work done for others? It is anything done with unselfishness and generosity—a putting aside (or overcoming) of ego for the benefit of another person.

But what if that other person is a jerk, a bad person who doesn't give a damn for you or your good work? So much more the need for the courage I could not muster as a paperboy and so much more the reason to try.

As Lao Tzu asks in the *Tao Te Ching,* "What is a good man but a bad man's teacher? What is a bad man but a good man's job?"

In previous books, I have described my skepticism of companies that make public their claims to conduct their business according to Christian principles, then use those "principles" to try to prescribe and control behavior and repress their employees rather than liberate and encourage them.

Some of these businesses include, usually before or after the workday, such activities as prayer groups or Bible study groups. That's hard to argue with, but I have never been convinced that, despite claims of no pressure, some employees won't feel coerced or pressured into participating. And those employees will be fearful of possible consequences of not participating. I've counseled employees in this situation. Yet I know of and respect business executives who do use their religious principles to guide them in honoring and liberating the human spirit and in empowering their employees.

There is obviously a certain uneasiness, a certain risk, in the subject of religion and business. Some of the risk is put to rest, I believe, by concentrating on the spirit in work, the opportunity it gives us to find personal and spiritual growth, rather than focusing on a particular sectarian interpretation of that spirituality.

But what does "spiritual growth" mean? I don't have a simple answer, and perhaps not even a good answer, but I believe spiritual growth has a lot to do with opportunities we have to connect on a deeper level with one another. I deeply want to believe we find easy connection through our shared joys, but I know in my heart that the connections come most readily from shared loss and pain, and that is because in times of pain there is usually nothing to say to one another except the obvious, which, I believe, leaves us searching for other expressions. Those expressions, if we are open to the opportunities, may make appropriate the things we usually find difficult: a touch, even a hug, tears, a long walk, a note with a poem enclosed, the assurance that we will be thinking about or praying for our colleague or friend or employee.

A lot of trivia drops away when someone says, "I have cancer," when someone's child is seriously ill, or when a loved one dies. The only thing to do in those circumstances is show you care. And that is not always easy to do.

This is not to say the possibilities for deeper connections come only in times of pain. There simply is no denying something ineffable in the act of working together to accomplish what we set out to accomplish. I believe we feel this something but often don't recognize it, much less understand how to express it. We can't even put labels on it. We say we "love" our jobs, we find them "challenging and reward-ing," we are "motivated," we are "team players," we take "pride" in what we do. Managers talk about "vision" and "excellence" and "qual-ity" and "empowerment." We coach and are coached; we mentor and are mentored; we seek continuous improvement; we want always to be learning. We talk about ethics and integrity, about health and healing. We have all this language, yet what does it literally say about the inde-finable something we feel about what we have chosen to do? Very little. The same is true as we try to express those feelings through par-ties and celebrations and conferences, through pep rallies and retreats, through the simple act of an informal get-together after work.

But those who are willing to take a more metaphorical view will find that these superficial words and activities symbolize the most pro-found expressions of our deepest selves, and they will understand that we simply have not developed an adequate vocabulary for what we feel as we seek meaning and dignity and growth in the everydayness of our work and lives.

Among my regrets as a manager is that I did not develop a clear enough sense of this metaphorical view in earlier years and, when I did, that I did not do more to help my colleagues and employees find that meaning in the work we did together.

It was not until the early eighties when I was a senior corporate executive that I began to understand the power of the spirit in work, the need for community and connection among workers, and the way work provides opportunity for growth of many kinds. Of course I had felt this power, but I didn't understand it well or know how to talk about it.

When I did begin to understand the need to find meaning in the everyday things, to see the divine in others, to discover holiness in the most mundane of activities, I wanted to know how to do these things. I began with the help of others to read about myth and Eastern religions, subjects about which I was colossally ignorant. I went to seminars and lectures and retreats. I became even more in touch with my spiritual roots and reestablished a deeper relationship with the religion of my childhood than I'd ever had or thought I'd have—a relationship informed by a deep appreciation of other religious practice.

I began also to know in my gut that the inner life must not be separated from the work we have chosen to do, no matter what that work is. I knew the only reasonable and healthy choice in work and life is to find the balance and, in turn, to help others find that balance. I realized that "burnout" is not a matter of working too hard but a matter of finding no meaning in what we do; not a problem of mental/physical energy but a problem of emotional energy; not a crisis of time but a crisis of spirit. As my pastor once put it, "It is not that we bite off more than we can chew, it's that we bite off more than we can savor."

More and more I came to know that what most of us need is not getting away from the drudgery of work but a getting into the joy of work, not a separation of life and work but an integration of life and work.

I quote Rabindranath Tagore:

I slept and dreamt that life was Joy;
and then I awoke and realized
that life was Duty.
And then I went to work—and, lo
and behold I discovered that
Duty can be joy.

These understandings or realizations or moments of truth pre-scribed for me a path that was quite different from the one most often used in business, particularly by senior corporate executives. Once again I found myself needing the courage to witness, and somehow it seemed more important than ever. Once I began, I found many fellow travelers and I found that virtually everything I had learned from my paperboy days through my Air Force days and into senior management pointed incontrovertibly in the same direction: toward the inside, toward the inner life, toward the ineffable.

There are many lessons about the spirit of work, and three of the most important are these: We should be thankful for work itself, we should be thankful for the people we work with, and we should be thankful for the grace of our spiritual possibilities at work.

So look, Mom, God rest your soul, I'm trying to witness.

Of Corporations and Communion

In a way,
the good people are still with us,
all those you can name
plus many you never knew.
They are part of this celebration
which as we know
is not about careers and accomplishments
but about life itself,
life and the two things that keep us living,
relationships and work,
the people we love and the things we love to do.
So, many of those who have gone before
are here,
and in a way,
so are the ones who are still to come,
even those not yet born.

"How can they be?" you ask.
Consider this:
Life and work and love in any setting,
even a corporation,

can be acts of communion
transcending all of us who pass through,
with our only hope being
that when we retire or take our leave,
we have left something of ourselves,
enough that part of us will be there always.
"And how do we do that?" you ask.

Listen.
Work, those things we have set ourselves to do,
is like everything else in life,
and our chance for immortality
comes only through what we have done
to help other people.
Some of us succeed, some of us don't.

If in a business enterprise we could,
as in the church,
attach special spiritual significance
to those who succeed,
if we could build shrines or dedicate holy places,
if we could but call them
teacher or master, prophet or saint,
there might be words available,
a vocabulary of praise we could use
to commemorate what they have done.
But we are reduced to this:
They will always be here.
And so, we pray,
may we all.

—from *Life and Work*, 1994

Chapter Seven

Where Are You Spending Eternity?

A friend used to say time is God's way of making us think everything doesn't happen at once. Which leads me to ask questions about eternity, how it's discussed in religious settings, and how we could think of it differently.

"Where do you plan to spend eternity?" the Southern Baptist preachers of my childhood used to ask. I heard a lot about "spending eternity in hell" or "dwelling with God in paradise." Naturally, given the opportunity, I'd choose the latter, and according to the preachers I was given that opportunity every day. All I had to do was profess Jesus as my personal savior, make a public confession of faith, be baptized, then wait for eternity, which meant, in other words, wait to die. So I dutifully did all that.

As I got older, however, I came to believe that I had wasted a lot of time waiting for eternity, because it dawned on me finally that eternity had already begun.

Remember the song "These Are the Good Old Days"? The same is true of eternity: we are already living in eternity. And indeed it may be hell for some of us—in fact, it has been hell for me from time to time—but I know also that paradise is still available. I know because it has come to me in the glimpses of wonder and mystery I've had and still have when I'm paying attention, living in the present, and trying to appreciate the time, minute by minute, left to me in this life.

So I believe this: If we can think of eternity as having already begun—and I do—and if we can find ways to be still and be open to the feast of beauty already here for us—and I try every day—and if we believe God is part of everything in this world—and I do—then we have but to recognize that there's no waiting. We can "dwell with God in paradise" right now, every day, every minute, as we live through this phase of eternity.

Questions for a Seventeen-year Cicada

Note: The Seventeen-year Cicada, upon hatching, drops to the ground and burrows into the earth where it stays as a larva for seventeen years, after which it makes it way to the surface, breaks open its shell, dries its wings, and flies into the trees. It remains there for a few weeks, feeding and singing its mating song incessantly throughout the day. Then it mates and lays its eggs under the bark of branches. The eggs hatch and the cycle begins again.

Were you surprised,
after waiting all those years,
to emerge still helpless
and struggling to find your wings
in this world
of birds with hungry beaks
and children with cruel fingers,
before you could fly up into the bliss
you had dreamed about?

Did it live up to the fantasies
that sustained you as you escaped
only by luck and position
those daily threats to your earthly life,
moles and snakes,
back hoes and cable trenchers
that would have untimely ripped you
from the larval womb?

And who told you to be so patient,
who promised that if you would just stay there,
content in the anonymity of clay,
you would one day shed your shell and,
glistening wet in a cloak of red and black and green,
rise in glory from the dust
to sing a love song the world had almost forgotten?

When at last you've answered those questions,
answer this one:
Which was better,
the solitude, the quiet life of patience and preparation,
or those final flights of ecstasy
within the community of lovers?

Chapter Eight

Chasing After a Miracle

It's probably true that you don't think about miracles much until you think you need one. At least I didn't. As a kid I wondered about the accuracy of biblical miracles, and I remember latching on to "scientific" explanations for such things as the parting of the Red Sea or Jesus walking on water, but I think I've really wanted a miracle only twice in my life. Once was when my brother was dying of cancer. I wanted one then. I prayed for one then.

Next was when my wife and I were told our then two-year-old son was diagnosed with autism. He's now twenty-two, and I wanted a miracle throughout most of those years. Beyond wanting a miracle, I chased after one. My operating philosophy was that if there was anything to try and I was assured it would do no harm, we'd try it. We'd take Ronald anywhere, do anything that might help him.

We took him to a doctor in New York who was well known for visualization therapy. Dr. E. told us it would help if we, my wife and I, would sit meditatively, close our eyes, and visualize things we wanted Ronald to do. Normal things, like ride a bike, throw and catch a ball, and so on. Sally had trouble visualizing, but I've always had an active fantasy life, with fully formed images in color and with music, so visualization was no trouble for me.

Another doctor said, "Take him off milk and dairy products." We did that for a while with no noticeable change.

We read that megavitamin therapy works with some children who have autism. We dutifully tried that. I must say that Ronald was very cooperative, probably more than I would have been, gulping down huge pills in huge quantities. After the prescribed period of time at which we should have noticed change, we didn't. So we stopped that therapy.

There is indication that some children with autism can be helped by taking a medicine that is commonly used to kill certain intestinal bacteria. An M.D. told us it would not be harmful and prescribed some. It didn't seem to work.

Then we decided to try psychic healing. I contacted friends who suggested a healer in Los Angeles. We tried two days of sessions. On the first day, the healer said he thought Ronald's spirit had not fully integrated with his body, that it was still, in effect, outside the body. Ronald was cooperative in these sessions.

The healer was a fastidious housekeeper, and that was to become a problem. His apartment seemed to be various shades of white and off-white, including the carpet. He even had one of those fluffy little white dogs that remind me of a noisy little pillow with four legs.

Ronald, who was not quite four years old at the time, loved the dog of course. The dog did not love him, however, and bit him lightly on the nose. It wasn't a bad bite but it did draw blood. Ronald started crying and screaming. It should be said that Ronald's reaction to pain, still to this day, is far out of proportion to the pain itself, making it difficult sometimes for us to determine how badly he is hurt.

The screaming made the dog bark, which only scared Ronald who undoubtedly thought the dog would bite him again. Perhaps because of the fear of being bitten or perhaps just because it was time, Ronald, who was not yet potty trained, had a bowel movement. He was in diapers, but, either because of volume or consistency, the diapers did not fully contain the deposit, a few small bits of which made their way onto the white carpet. The psychic healer became very unspiritual, rushing around with paper towels and detergents. Sally and Ronald and I took our leave. It didn't seem that the psychic healing worked either.

My only regret was that I hadn't managed to give a swift kick to the dog or the healer or both. Though it did seem to me some sort of appropriate recompense that Ronald had managed to shit on the white carpet. This sounds funnier than it was.

I realize now that there was a measure of desperation in all these attempts to find a "cure," and the psychic healing episode was only moderately more desperate than the others.

This stretched over several years, and throughout all this time I was praying. I've read the articles and studies on intercessional prayer and healing, and I convinced myself that everything we were doing, from the visualization to the dietary supplements (oh yes, those too) was just another form of prayer, another way of appealing to the great unknown to hand us down a ready-made miracle.

I never expected anything sudden, like Lazarus waking up and climbing out of the tomb. If it happened at all, I expected a slow-motion miracle. I expected Ronald to accelerate in his learning, his motor skills, his social skills, his communication skills. Just steady progress on a curve that would some day catch him up with his peers.

Not that we were ignoring all the conventional interventions, medical and educational. Part of the diagnostic progress had been to take Ronald to an eminent medical facility in New York, where he was seen by one of the leading pediatric neurologists in the country.

The first time we took him, when he was about two and a half years old, Dr. R. said, "I really don't know what scale to put this child on. I'm not sure what the diagnosis should be, but probably autism." She told us she did not know how he'd do mentally and that he might never talk. Then she told us to bring him back the next year.

Shortly after we returned with Ronald to our home in Des Moines, we met a public school teacher acquaintance at a party. We told her about Ronald and the trip to New York. Of course we told everyone at that time about Ronald; he was heavy on our minds. She asked if we'd considered signing him up for the infant intervention program of the public schools. We'd never heard of if but called the next day.

In a few days, a teacher from the public schools came to our home, and after talking with us and observing Ronald a while, she sat on the floor, positioned him in front of her, and began to teach him to play with blocks, saying words as she did so.

She said she'd come once a week and then would sign him up for a class the following fall when he was not quite three years old.

The next week she began to teach him, and us, elementary sign language. He and we learned "more," "milk," "cookie," and other helpful words.

Something clicked. Whenever Ronald would sign a word, we'd respond appropriately, and his face would light up. He had been understood at last.

A few months after that, he spoke his first word. I had made up a little song that had the repetitive refrain "His name is Ronald." My habit was to sing "His name is Ronald" during the refrain over and over and then on the final time sing "His name is_____" and wait for him. And finally he did it. He said something approximating "Ronald." Reflecting on the meaning of the word "autism," it's even more understandable, as well as interesting, that his first word was his own name and not "Mama" or "Dada."

When fall came, he boarded a yellow school bus every morning and rode to a school across town, where he was in a class with five other autistic boys, a teacher, and two aides.

The next summer, we took him back to the doctor in New York. After about five minutes, she asked, with what I thought was considerable incredulity, "What have you done with this child?" We told her about the school program. Then she said something I felt was the most forthcoming thing any of Ronald's doctors had said: "Mr. and Mrs. Autry, you pay attention to those educators. They know much more about these children than we do."

From that point on, we continued our sometimes desperate quest for a miracle, as described above, but we also put our main efforts into supporting the public school teachers and therapists. And we tried to turn every experience into a learning experience. Ronald went to music therapy, and then later when he seemed interested in drums, he took drum lessons. He went on to play in the high school band.

He has a way with animals, so when we heard of a woman who did horseback therapy ("hippotherapy") with mentally disabled children, we signed him up. He did that once a week for several years, and for ten years we've spent a week every year at a wonderful horse ranch in Colorado.

Ronald has pretty good computer skills. He has always been obsessed with airplanes and cuckoo clocks and now goes on eBay to look over, and sometimes bid on, his favorite clocks and model airplanes.

So what am I trying to say? Just this: With all that we tried, I believe we'll never know what worked and what didn't. Maybe none of it. Maybe all of it, even the psychic healing. But I don't waste time trying to analyze it. I do know that at some point while chasing after the one big miracle, I finally recognized the real miracle workers and realized that miracles are happening almost every day, one person at a time, one teacher, one friend, one family member, one coach, one music teacher, one ranch-hand wrangler, and one parent at a time.

Would I still like a big gift from God, a sudden, dramatic miracle that would help Ronald's future life, that would help him realize our two ambitions for him: to live independently and to have a love relationship?

Yes, of course, but I'm not desperate about it because, at the same time, I recognize that the greatest gift, the biggest miracle, and in fact the most successful miracle worker in all of this is Ronald himself. And really, what more could I ask?

Something Like a Prayer

Ronald sleeps hotter than any boy I know
(a phrase he likes, as in
"You have more airplanes than any boy I know")
and scrunched into the twist of sheet and quilt
sweats everything wet within the first hour.
Every night I rearrange the covers,
straightening and flattening them
so he can breathe,
then sit on his bed
and press my face against his head,
wondering sometimes if his dreams
are filled like his life

with a million questions and no understanding,
and close my eyes into images of things
I want him to do,
ride a bike, catch a ball,
speak in regular boy tones,
sending my mind pictures
through his wet hair and into his dreams,
making this ritual something like a prayer
that one morning he will awaken
and live with me in this world.

Chapter Nine

Mystical Blessings

Bill Connet, a musician with a religious calling, regularly entertains elderly residents in assisted care facilities. It's a simple procedure: the people make their way, or are wheeled, into the "activity room." Bill talks a bit, plays the guitar, and sings. Then it's over. An ordinary event for Bill, a special treat for the residents.

But on one day when Bill was expecting to do a mini concert not unlike the others, something happened that made this performance create possibilities he could not have imagined.

One of the residents was an eighty-six-year-old woman named Irene. She seemed listless and unfocused; Bill, who had spent several years in health care administration, recognized the symptoms of dementia. He smiled and nodded to her as she was placed in the front row. He received no response.

This day could have been a day and a performance like any other day and performance, pleasant and entertaining and personally fulfilling for Bill, but about halfway through his lineup of old songs and new compositions, he suddenly felt moved to do something he'd not done before: he played "Amazing Grace."

"The change in the room was palpable," he says, "and suddenly Irene began to move her lips and then sing, the words clearly articulated and her high and thin voice right on pitch. The other people, especially the caregivers, were stunned; they'd never heard her speak."

From "Amazing Grace" Bill moved to "Jesus Loves Me." The room became livelier, and Irene continued to sing. "It felt like an old-time revival meeting, only a quieter, slower version," he says.

Now Bill regularly plays the old hymns because he realizes they somehow reach beyond the dementia to a deeper place. Bill does not try to explain the mysterious connections the old hymns make with his audience.

Just as I can't explain the mystical things that seem to happen to me regularly. Surely they've happened to you also.

I recall years ago, freshly back from military service in France as an Air Force jet fighter pilot, I was driving—faster than I should as usual—with my first wife and our two small sons on a hilly two-lane highway in Tennessee.

As we started up a steep hill, I accelerated in order to keep up my speed. I was always in a hurry when traveling. It was a blind hill and as I neared the top, there was a sign warning of a crossroads, a sign that would cause most cautious drivers to let up on the accelerator and perhaps even prepare to brake. I was not at that time a cautious driver. But just short of the top of the hill, for reasons I could not explain later to my wife or to myself, I slammed the brakes hard, just short of skidding. As we topped the hill, braking rapidly, my wife and sons thrown forward—there were no seatbelts then—we saw a hay wagon being pulled by a tractor. It had pulled out onto the highway from a side road, and there was a car was in the oncoming lane. Had we not been decelerating, we would have slammed into the wagon at a disastrous speed. But I managed to keep the car under control and maneuver to the shoulder where, after stopping, we sat for several minutes. The boys were crying, and both my wife and I were shaking.

I know everyone has a story like this. They are so common, in fact, that people hardly consider them worth telling anymore. But in this case, there was clearly no apparent reason for me to have hit the brakes. I even took time to look for clues—dust, hay on the road, anything—but there was no explanation.

When I told my father about it, his explanation was predictable. "God was telling you to slow down, Boy."

I really don't think God was telling me to slow down, giving me an "or else" warning. That's a far too fundamentalist, his-eye-is-on-the-sparrow belief for me. Yet it clearly was a mystical experience, and I do think of myself as a mystical Christian and look for God within things not easily explained.

About fifteen years ago I was flying a small plane over Missouri, from Tennessee to Iowa, when an oil line burst and my engine froze up. Suddenly my plane had become a glider. I called an FAA flight service station and declared a mayday. It was not a particularly hazardous situation in that I was over flat wheat fields and figured I could make a reasonably safe landing.

At first the FAA person said I should land on the interstate highway. That seemed too great a risk.

"No," I said, "I'll try to put it in a wheat field or a pasture if I can find one."

At that time, another voice came on the radio. He called my plane number and said, "I'm a local pilot and I have you in sight. If you can make it across the interstate, there's a cotton duster strip just east of it." I looked across the interstate and saw a trailer with a windsock standing at the edge of an unmowed pasture. It didn't look like a runway, but I headed for it. I had enough altitude and speed and made a safe forced landing.

I got out of the plane and pushed it to the side of the field, then walked slowly toward the trailer. On the side of the trailer was the name of this tiny airport: "Holyfield."

I've become drawn more and more to the mystical in our lives. I've read a lot about the ESP experiments and have talked with people who study the research closely. I guess I admire the effort to explain the unknown and even to try to replicate the experiences, but I think we non-scientists might be better served simply to accept that these things happen and be open to them as part of the great mystery we call life.

A few years ago, several months after the death of Susie, my beloved sister-in-law, I was in Atlanta on business and decided to stop by the church memorial garden where her ashes were scattered. As I was walking slowly and meditatively along the winding path through the azaleas and pines, I heard my sister-in-law's voice. "Jimmy," she called. "Are you here?" It was as surreal an experience as I've ever had, frightening almost.

I hurried around the next bend and saw a woman. It was not Susie but one of her best friends whom I'd met on many occasions. Her voice has the same timbre, same inflections, same rhythm as Susie's voice. She ran to me and we hugged. After a few moments of tears, she said, "Jimmy, I dreamed last night about Susie. She appeared to me and said, 'I'm still with you.' This morning, I felt a very strong pull to visit this place. I've not been here in a long time, and when I saw your name on the registry, it made me shiver. I guess you and I were supposed to be here together today."

I guess so too.

It's easy to call these experiences simple coincidences, nothing special, nothing to marvel at. But I think that, for some reason, we are uncomfortable with the mysterious and even uncomfortable with the idea of synchronicity, thus we are impelled to find a rational explanation for everything that happens. That's okay for scientists, and I don't suggest that we reject scientific explanations. But I submit that such explanations don't illuminate the incidents I've described here or the ones I believe you also have experienced.

So I prefer to accept these everyday happenings as simply mysterious and to call them what they are to me: blessings.

Messages

It was during that long wailing ambulance ride to Memphis
after the heart attack
she dreamed about her brothers,
killed those forty years ago
working on the railroad.
Not dreamed about them exactly
but about looking at their pictures,
studying their young and arrogant railroad man faces,
then noticing another picture frame,
empty and blank,
saved for her,
a sign it was not yet time for her to go.
So, she told me later,
she relaxed and enjoyed the trip.

Meanwhile trying to keep up with the ambulance
in my rental car
I heard the urgent whistle of a train
and looked to see it running parallel with the highway,
staying even with us.
Painted on the side of the freight cars
was some kind of slogan,
an advertising slogan I'm sure,
stretched along the train,
car after car,
saying simply
We're pulling for you
We're pulling for you
We're pulling for you . . .

—Adapted from *Confessions of An Accidental Businessman*, 1996

Chapter Ten

Prayer for a Country Preacher

When as a child I spent time with my father in North Mississippi, during the 1940s and 1950s, we always had dogs around the yard. Never in the house as people do today, but around the yard. Hound dogs and bird dogs and terriers. We kept the hounds and the bird dogs penned up mostly, calling on them only for hunting, our major source of meat. The terriers, not a purebred among them but always smart little dogs, were for treeing squirrels and keeping away varmints, especially foxes that might catch the chickens and snakes who would either get the chicken eggs or, worse, bite us.

The dogs probably were not healthy by today's standards. They ate table scraps, dead animals, most anything they could find that was edible. Usually one or the other of them was suffering some sort of malady: worms or the mange. For the most part, they were fairly sorry-looking dogs by dog-show standards. But lovable and dependable.

As a kid, I'd play with them. Or try to. During the hot summer, they'd spend a lot of time sleeping in the shade, and I liked to watch them because they sometimes barked or groaned in their sleep. Often, as if running, they'd move their legs and bark a sort of far-off bark.

One day, I was watching one older dog running and barking in her sleep, and Dad paused behind me and said, "Boy, that old dog is dreaming she's chasing a rabbit. She's having a big time." And he laughed.

I remembered that day years later, only a few weeks before my father's death, as I stood watching him sleep. He began to smile and his lips began to move. He became almost animated, not speaking clearly but his voice rising and falling in volume as if emphasizing certain words or phrases. I thought to myself but said to no one, "That old preacher is dreaming he's preaching a sermon."

A few days later, I wrote this poem:

Prayer for a Country Preacher

Oh God
let him go dreaming when he goes
let him go preaching a revival meeting
with the congregation eager beyond discomfort
on a wet and insect-laden night

let him go singing bass
on a Sunday morning
his head above the others
his voice bringing power beyond
power in the blood

let him go walking the river bottom
leading the lost fishermen through the storm
breaking saplings to mark the trail

let him go wading the shallows
his boots sucking mud in the dawn
calling the green-headed mallard
shooting quick and sure
    Not bad for a country preacher

let him go praying
at a table of summer Sunday food
fried chicken and sliced tomatoes
and peas and cornbread and tea

with his family around him
like disciples

Oh God if he must go
let him go dreaming.

—from *Nights Under a Tin Roof*, 1983

Chapter Eleven

Angels Everywhere

"Do not forget to entertain strangers, for by so doing some people have entertained angels without knowing it." —Hebrews 13:2

I'm inclined to add to this Scripture my belief that it might also be true that some of us have been entertained by angels and not known it. I'm inclined also to expand the definition of "entertained" beyond hospitality to include "greeted," "helped," "comforted," "rescued," and so on.

What is required for us to recognize these angels who, it is said, are all around us? Perhaps it's simply an open heart. Surely it involves abandoning our expectations about what angels might look like or how they might announce themselves. And I think it also requires a special lens, or a prism, through which we are more likely to know angels when we see them.

My lens, or prism, is my son with a disability. Since Ronald came into my life, angels have been popping up everywhere, and I've come to know them when I see them. Oh, I never say, "There goes an angel," and I never tell the angels I know who they are. They wouldn't want me to. But I acknowledge them to myself and am always grateful for their blessing.

Let me give you some examples.

When Ronald was about two and a half years old, we were told, after many tests, that he had autism. Thanks to an infant early intervention and preschool program in the Des Moines public schools, he began to go to school when he was not yet three years old.

Every morning, we would put him on a yellow school bus with a group of other children, all of whom had disabilities of one sort or another. Every afternoon, he would return on the bus. One day I was home from the office and met the bus. I had heard about the bus driver, a man the children called "Toad," but had never met him.

As Ronald got off the bus, Toad said, "Goodbye, Ronald, I'll see you tomorrow." Ronald was not yet verbal. He had some minimal sign language but could pronounce only the first sound of a word. For "Bye," he said something like "Buh," which came out as little more than the "B" sound itself. That was all he could say.

I learned that day that he and Toad had a ritual. After Ronald, who had motor skill problems as well, climbed laboriously down the school bus steps, he turned. Toad said again, "Bye, Ronald."

Ronald said, "Buh," and smiled.

Toad said, "Look at me, Ronald." Eye contact is difficult for many people with autism, and they must be encouraged and taught to make eye contact. "Look at me, Ronald," Toad said.

Ronald looked at him. Toad looked at Ronald, making full eye contact, and said "I love you, Ronald."

Imagine that. This big school bus driver, every single school day, would engage my little boy's attention and say, "I love you, Ronald." I can't imagine that Ronald experienced anything at school in those days more important than his relationship with Toad.

I've tried to imagine also what instinct, what knowledge, what wisdom moved Toad to make those connections with the children, many of whom would barely acknowledge or were barely able to acknowledge him. I know Toad would never have thought of himself as an angel and would have been embarrassed had I said such a thing, but he was one nonetheless, as surely as there are angels, sent to bring love and dignity and a positive human relationship to little children whose disabilities would probably always make those kinds of relationships difficult.

I suspect angels know when to be present and know what they're supposed to do. Ronald's first teacher, Twyla Wanek, had never been trained about how to relate to children with autism. "I learned it the hard way," she said. "When I first started working with these children, no one even used the word 'autism.' No one talked about autism at all; maybe they didn't know what it was. I was just told that these kids were mentally retarded or had a behavior disorder, or some combination. So I just started teaching them and worked it out for myself."

When I first visited her class, "Wanek" (as the children called her) was down on her knees gently restraining a boy whose behavior had become overly aggressive—not an uncommon event in a class of children with autism. She was firm in overpowering him in a way that would prevent his hurting himself or someone else, yet she was gentle and loving.

My most enduring impression of Twyla is that she was never still. She was on the floor or moving from child to child—speaking in her constantly upbeat, encouraging voice, always reinforcing the sometimes meager accomplishments of a struggling student: job!" or "Look at me. Good looking." She taught every single second of the day.

I believe she knew and felt deeply that whole futures depended on her willingness to do this work and on her energy in accomplishing it. And it took more physical and emotional stamina than most of us can imagine bringing to any job. If I didn't know that angels must have an extra quotient of what it takes, I would wonder how Wanek did it for so many years.

A final story about Ronald: A few years ago, my beloved sister-in-law Susie, Ronald's aunt, was stricken with pancreatic cancer. She decided against extraordinary measures to keep her alive and moved into a hospice facility. Ronald wanted to visit her before her inevitable death, so I booked the two of us on a flight to Atlanta.

While standing in line waiting our turn at the ticket counter, my cell phone rang. It was my nephew; Susie had died a few minutes before.

When I told Ronald the news and also told him we would not go that day but would arrange tickets for us, as well as for my wife, Sally, to go the next day, he went crazy. Changes of routine or schedule are difficult for most people with autism. In this case, Ronald was facing a schedule change plus the reality of his aunt's death plus the sadness of not getting to see her alive again before she died.

His behavior was beyond troublesome. He was crying and screaming and insisting that we were going to Atlanta anyway. When he was a child, this behavior could happen at any time and in any place—the grocery store, at church, anywhere—but since he had become a teenager, the behavior had grown more moderate. Now, though, it was as if he'd reverted to the tantrums of childhood. Other passengers in line stared at us, which only made the behavior worse. There was nothing I could do but try to calm him and understand that he felt as sad as I felt but didn't have the mechanisms to react calmly.

When we made our way to the passenger agent, she was extraordinarily calm and courteous. I explained the situation, telling her about the death and our need for tickets the next day to the funeral. Ronald kept interrupting, screaming and crying and trying to talk me into going as originally scheduled. The passenger agent seemed relaxed, not rushed, even though other people were behind us in line. She cancelled our two tickets then wrote three new ones for the next day, calmly and methodically doing all the paperwork as if nothing out of the ordinary was happening.

Ronald walked away while she was finishing the transaction, and I said, "I really appreciate your help. I'm sorry for the disturbance, but truthfully he's only reacting to the news the way I'd like to react myself." She looked at me with unmistakable compassion, and said, "That's okay. I understand. In my other job, I'm a special ed teacher and work regularly with kids with autism. I only work part-time for the airline."

Only part-time for the airline, but she just happened to be on duty when Ronald and I arrived and just happened to be the agent when our turn came for assistance. Who could she have been but an angel?

Because of Ronald, I have become sensitive to the presence of people with disabilities. A few days ago, I followed a young man with a mental disability in line at the supermarket. When the cashier, an attractive young woman, rang the total, $10.86, he handed her a ten-dollar bill. "Ten eighty-six," she said. The young man looked confused, then said, "I have ten dollars."

The cashier smiled. "Okay," she said, then reached under the counter and pulled out her purse. "I have a dollar," she said. I was amazed.

Then I reached in my pocket for some change and pulled out all I had, exactly eighty-six cents (I'm not making this up) and put it on the counter. "Save your dollar," I said, "I have the change."

The young man seemed not to know what had transpired, but took his groceries and left.

"Do you know him?" I asked the cashier.

"No," she said, "I just see him in here every once in a while."

"Well, that was a generous and supportive thing you were about to do."

She shrugged. "Everyone runs short of change sometimes."

Think about that a minute. The cashier herself was probably being paid eight dollars or so an hour, yet she was about to give her own money to help this young man out of an embarrassing and confusing situation.

Am I saying every random act of kindness is a sign of angels? Yes. Either that or the people I've described take the Scripture seriously, expressing these kindnesses because they know they may be "entertaining" angels.

Of course there's even another way to look at it: Doesn't Scripture teach that we are all given the opportunity in this life not only to entertain angels but to become angels ourselves?

On Paying Attention

There came a time in my volunteer life
when I began to give in
to the seductions of righteousness
and to think of my work as a sacrifice
for the good of others.
I would make schedules no one should try
so that people would ask
how it was possible for one man to do so much.
It was a time of three speeches
and three cities
in one day,

and in all the scurrying
I did not want the delay
of a restroom conversation
with a hesitant little man
in a cheap new suit.
I needed a quick pee, five minutes to think,
and two minutes to get to the podium.
But there he was,
with the side effects I knew so well,
the puffy cheeks, the swollen gums
as he smiled and told me he had a job now
and hadn't had a seizure in six months.
I gave him the quick back pat
and the smile,
never expecting to see him again.
But he sat in the front row
and smiled a greeting when I rose to speak,
the dignitary from the national office,
bringing word from Washington,
the National Commission,
the Hill, the White House.
He smiled too often
and over-nodded and made too much of his notes,
clicking his pen and turning pages,
back and forth,
as if studying what he'd written.
When our eyes met he smiled and nodded,
another guy, I thought, who wants people
to think he knows the speaker.
So I avoided looking at him
until he shuffled, crossed his legs,
and stretched them in front of him.
When I saw the soles of his shoes,
slightly soiled, less than a day worn,
I realized he had bought the suit and shoes
just for this meeting,

just to hear a speech squeezed
into an afternoon between two other cities.
He had looked forward to it,
planned for it,
put new job money into it,
and would make notes
so that he could remember always
what the important man came to teach.
But the lesson was mine to learn—
about sacrifice
and counting blessings,
about patience
and paying attention to teachers
wherever I find them.

—from *Life After Mississippi*, 1989

Chapter Twelve

Unexpected Communion

William Stafford, the great Kansas poet, once said that the poet's work is to dig so deep into his own story that he reaches everyone's story.

A few years ago, in performing an activity as elder of my church, I found myself reaching individual stories in a way that was both surprising and revelatory. My job was to deliver Communion to older people who could no longer make it to church. "Shut-ins," they're commonly called.

What I experienced was a different kind of communion, a communion that was not intended but that took on an unexpected importance both for me and for the people I was serving. It was a rich and humbling experience that, as I try to record it, seems more appropriate to express in poetry rather than prose.

Taking Communion to the Shut-ins

It was a weekly duty of the elders
after regular church service in the sanctuary
to pack up the little boxes of bread
and the jugs of grape juice,
to get my list from the church office
and to visit the old and infirm,
aged and aging members who still lived at home,
and for whom the weekly Eucharist
had become so much a part of their lives
that to miss it one week would be to create
an unredeemable absence.

It was a simple routine, a greeting, a prayer,
the eating of the bread and drinking of the juice,
some parting pleasantries and on to the next one.
But it turned out not to be so easy
because of the stories and not just the stories
but how I became part of the stories,
an old fishing buddy, a son, a brother, a husband, a lost lover.
"You walk quick the way my husband used to walk;
my Daddy wondered why I would marry a man who walked so
quick."

I became not so much a messenger from the church
as a messenger from time and out of time,
resurrected for a few minutes into someone's main character,
changing from story to story
so at the end of the day I felt as if I had been found and lost,
celebrated and mourned,
over and over again,
yet helpless to be more than a witness
to the desperate attempt we all make
to understand the great mystery
of presence within absence.

Chapter Thirteen

What about Those Close Calls?

There's probably not a present or former military pilot alive who has not had a share of close calls. I only flew for four and a half years in the Air Force, yet I had plenty of close calls, some more memorable than others.

Once while flying an F-86 Sabrejet at only 100 feet above the ground over agricultural fields in Morocco, I made an almost fatal mistake. I didn't have much experience flying low at high speeds. My flight leader had said, "Do everything I do," so when he did an aileron roll, I did too. The only problem was that I hadn't pulled the nose up before rolling. The next thing I knew I was upside down and so low that I could identify the crops as cotton. Somehow I managed to roll out without my wingtip hitting the ground. It scared my flight leader, who not only screamed into the radio but also chewed me out once I was back at the base.

On another occasion I had to make a landing in an F-100 Supersabre in fog and smoke at a base in England. I was so low on fuel that I was unable to go anywhere else. I saw the runway lights a split second before my wheels touched. And there was the time I accidentally flew into a thunderstorm that peeled back the metal skin on the airplane's wings and knocked out all my radios and navigational equipment.

Why was I not killed? We pilots knew that what was most likely to keep us alive were our skills and training, but we also talked about luck. Some of us were superstitious to the extent that we always wore the same flying boots or scarf, went through the same personal rituals or habits before flying, repeated the same prayers, made the same jokes.

Even though, like many of the pilots, I considered myself "religious" and attended chapel from time to time, I don't think grace ever entered my mind as a factor. When a pilot got killed, an inevitability from time to time in military flying, I never heard any pilot say God had a role in the accident.

That's why I am so perplexed by people who, after surviving an accident in which other people are killed, claim that God saved them. Not only that, but God saved them for a "purpose," thus God must have a special plan for them. I find myself wanting to shout, "So what about those other folks? Did God decide to let them die because He didn't have a special purpose or plan for them? If so, is that the kind of God you are comfortable believing in?"

This is not to say prayers of gratitude are not good and appropriate in these situations. Also, this is not to say that when we come through a threatening situation unscathed, we should not ask ourselves, "Why me?" Here's the difference, in my opinion: saying, "God spared me and let the others die because He has a plan and purpose for me" seems like an utterly egocentric response and also one in which the person is now imposing on God the responsibility to "reveal" the purpose.

With a better attitude, we might say, "I am thankful to God that I am still here and was not killed or maimed. This has given me yet another chance to examine how I am choosing to live my life, another opportunity to be sure that I have discovered and am fulfilling my purpose on this earth. I am saddened by the deaths of those who did not survive this terrible episode. They no longer have the opportunity I still have; this in itself intensifies my own moral obligation to assure that the rest of my life is on the track it should be."

The real lesson we should all take from close calls, ours or others', is that we should always seek our purpose and fulfill the promise of our lives, whether or not we have close brushes with death. After all, we are dying even as we are living. The only difference is circumstance and timing.

Jeopardy

I

How many times have I died?
At least once on the motorcycle,
with Jack Spencer on the back,
the unexpected cars
and the boy on the bicycle
and nothing to do but skid and hope

Or run off the road
by the Cadillac passing on the hill
outside Holly Springs.

And certainly in the F-86
over the cotton fields below Rabat
with Dickie on the radio,
"Jesus, Cowboy, pull up before you roll!"
(Think of that,
of all the hoeing and picking,
of all the sun hot hours in cotton fields
to hang my wing
and tumble into pieces
on some foreigner's cotton
ten thousand miles from my people's land.)

And in the fog at Wethersfield
in an Englishman's pasture
with sheep like gray boulders
in a wash of green
only a hundred yards from the runway
but far enough that all I could say
was Oh shit.

And in the whistling silence
of a dead engine.
And in a thunderstorm
that rolled back and wrinkled the metal skin
like an old-time cigarette paper
And in a hundred things I didn't even know about.

II

There are courts of inquiry somewhere,
accident investigators piecing it together.
There are coroners,
there are undertakers trying to make me
look okay after all.
There are caskets shipped back
filled with rubber sacks
not nearly full enough.
There are honor guards clicking their heels
and firing rifles in country cemeteries.
There are proud mothers
and wet-eyed widows
and children with pictures for fathers.

III

But through all those deaths,
I am here,
still and again,
with at least one to go,
and the only thing changed
is the limb I am out on.

Chapter Fourteen

Finding Bible Stories at the Movies

As a journalism and English major in college, I was exposed to allegory, symbolism, metaphor, and all that, but I confess I did not fully understand in my younger days how the true richness of literature lies not only in the story on the surface but in the story beneath the story.

This is not to deny that many good stories are only what they appear to be: good stories, page-turners, potboilers, grabbers. I read them and I enjoy them. But what intrigues me most these days are stories that operate on different levels, and most particularly those that tell age-old stories or explore age-old themes in new ways that bring other dimensions or provoke different thinking about the original.

In the occasional adult classes I lecture, I encourage people to open themselves to the possibility of the story beneath the story. This is also one of the reasons I believe strongly in biblical literacy, that we need to continue to teach the Bible stories. In fact, I believe people who are not familiar with the Bible stories, in both the Old and New Testaments, are depriving themselves of a body of knowledge that often informs and illuminates Western literature.

Lately, I've paid specific attention to the movies and regularly find themes I identify as "Christian." They include a person dying to save others; people finding redemption and healing through the sacrifice or leadership of another; resurrection; selfless service; and so on.

I'm not talking about overtly religious movies whose purpose is to tell the specific Christian story again, only with spectacular special effects. I'm talking about movies you might never think of as "Christian."

For example, take a look at *E. T.—The Extra Terrestrial*. It's a kids' movie that works for adults; it's something of a pot-boiler; it's a chase movie; it's a comedy; it's a drama. But look deeper and think about it.

From the heavens comes a creature, not exactly human but with distinct human characteristics. This creature is befriended by children, who as we know are capable of a special kind of faith, the "faith of a child" as the Bible says.

This alien creature, this very different person impresses the children with how "smart" he is; he even turns out to be a teacher to his young disciples. With his special touch, he heals a cut on the boy's finger. And he performs other miracles. Using various sizes of balls, he simulates the solar system to explain that he came from the heavens beyond that system. He sets up a way to communicate with his "home" ("E.T., phone home"). As he remains on earth, he knows he will come to no good end and must return to his heavenly parents.

Then the authorities find him. Sound familiar? He is already suffering from the effects of this world, and the authorities imprison him in a "tomb." All his life signs disappear, and, in effect, he dies. As his main friend walks away, flowers in a pot suddenly bloom, signaling another miracle. The friend quickly conspires with the other disciples to remove the body from the tomb with the intention of freeing E.T. to return to his home.

Then there is another miracle, the memorable scene in which the boys on their bicycles suddenly fly, escaping the authorities. They arrive safely at the appointed place where the resurrected E.T. says goodbye and ascends to be with his heavenly parents. So what will the boys do then? They'll tell the stories, of course: how he healed the wound, how he communicated in a different way with his heavenly parents; how he made them all fly. Those stories will live forever.

Does this sound like a bit of a stretch? Some people with whom I've shared this think so, but I contend it is a resurrection story and, in effect, a Christian allegory.

But why would Steven Spielberg, a Jew, make such a movie? I'm not sure, but I believe we are all so imbued with these ancient stories that they exist somewhere in the subconscious without connection to a particular faith or belief. And of course, similar stories existed in the Jewish tradition before the birth of Jesus. Or maybe Mr. Spielberg didn't intend any of it; maybe I'm projecting my own bias into the movie. But think about it.

How about *Cool Hand Luke*, the famous prison film starring Paul Newman? It's not a resurrection story, but it is certainly a story of a man who questions authority, who comforts his fellow prisoners, who works his own kind of miracles (prodigious eating of boiled eggs, prison escapes), and constantly tells stories and teaches the other prisoners. He also sets an example of how to live despite the oppressive environment. When the authorities finally kill him, the last scenes in the movie show the other prisoners (disciples?) telling his story over and over again so that his life and feats live on in the mythology of that place.

One more, fairly overlooked movie was also one of the most religious—the Tommy Lee Jones movie *The Three Burials of Melquiades Estrada*. See it. It is clearly a Christian allegory, and one of the most intriguing movies you'll find.

The plot is simple: A redneck border guard accidentally shoots and kills Melquiades Estrada, a Mexican illegally in the United States who is a friend of Pete Perkins, played by Jones. Subsequently, Perkins searches out and kidnaps the border guard, a young man who is angry, hostile, and obsessed with persecuting the "wetbacks." Perkins makes the young man dig up Estrada's body. He intends to fulfill a promise to Estrada to see that he is buried in a special place in Mexico, a place Estrada described to Perkins but that Perkins has never seen. Thus the movie is basically a "road trip" with Perkins, his prisoner, and the body of Melquiades, traveling by horse to Mexico.

The movie is filled with so much symbolism that I've been amazed that no critic mentions it. The real journey obviously is one from evil to redemption, a journey of spiritual growth and discovery. Before the trip, the young man is spiritually bereft, mired in a combination of working-class American materialism and a desolate job in which his symbols of power are expressed in violence toward Mexican migrants.

Even sex with his wife is expressed as male dominance: passionless, loveless, unconnected. He is, in a word, "lost."

The journey begins when the older wise man, Perkins, forces the young border guard to dig up Melquiades' body, to "resurrect" him, to take him and leave the tomb empty. The young man is then taken to Melquiades' house, where he is made to drink from the man's cup and put on his garments.

Then begins the journey through the wilderness. At one point, a rattlesnake bites the border guard. This symbolizes his confronting his own evil and sin. He's scared, wounded, and poisoned; he wants to be healed. On the way to find a healer, Perkins drags the young man through a river. This clearly is a baptism.

But the man is still filled with poison. They find the healer, a Mexican woman who sees him as evil and at first refuses to heal him. Earlier, when she was trying to cross the border, the young guard had broken her nose. She finally agrees to treat him, but then after the healing, she breaks his nose as he broke hers. This is an eye for an eye, Old Testament kind of justice.

After this episode, there is a point at which the border guard sees a group of people shucking corn. They are preparing the communal meal and he, haltingly and with obvious humility, joins in the preparation. From this point in the movie, he is a changed man but not yet fully redeemed.

When the two men finally arrive at the place Melquiades has described, they find not a paradise but a ruin where a ranch once stood. Yet Perkins sees the place as Melquiades saw it and describes it: "Mountains, good water." The young man then says softly, "You found it . . . . Yep, you found it." He says this with a tone of affirmation, reassurance, and affection. The subtle change here is that the border guard has become a giver, not a taker.

In the closing scenes, the men construct what is obviously a shrine. They bury the body. Then Perkins commands the young man to kneel before the symbolic altar and ask Melquiades to forgive him. He hesitates. Jones shoots several shots around him and symbolically kills him from this life. In fear and then in sincere repentance, the young man, kneeling and weeping in front of the altar, begs forgiveness.

Finally, he is left to himself, redeemed to a new life. His last words to the older wise man are words of concern, symbolizing that he is now thinking of others beyond himself.

Even though I've gone into much detail, there is far more to this film than I can adequately describe here. My point is simply to illustrate how rich and textured even a movie can become if you look for the story underneath the story, the story the critics will rarely recognize or, if they do, won't admit.

I know there's a lot of junk out there in the movie theaters, but I'm suggesting that there are films worth a second, deeper look. You might be surprised by what you begin to see. You might even find your faith affirmed and feel an appreciation for yet another way of telling the stories you already know so well.

Section Two:

Looking Unconventionally at the Church

Chapter Fifteen

Preach the Whole Story (and Treat Me Like a Grown-up)

I love the Christmas story and everything that surrounds it: grand music, candlelight worship services, carols, pageants, manger scenes, all of it. Never mind that the wise men and the shepherds didn't show up at the same time, and that as far as the Scriptures go, the wise men never even saw the manger. Nonetheless, the crèche still looks good on the mantel.

But I confess I get a little tired of all the minister talk about "anticipation." I don't like being told that this is the time we must be patient as we await the arrival of the child. This is a "time of waiting, a time of hope," and so on. At some point, it gets to be like a children's game into which all the adults must be drawn. I want to say, "Come on, guys, He made it here 2,000 years ago. I'm not still waiting."

I appreciate the metaphor of the light coming into the world. I participate in the worship services, and I love the basic story we Christians have concocted over the years, even if I have to suspend my disbelief and accept the conventional wise men/shepherds/manger story at face value. Nonetheless, in the past several years, I've experienced a growing interest in the life of Jesus and especially some of the supposedly historical episodes as well as the parables. It's not that I'm trying to become a theologian—far from it—but I increasingly want to reexamine some of what I've been taught in six decades as a Christian.

Frankly, some of it has made me resent the way I learned—and subsequently have understood—these things. I've begun to feel that, for most of my life as a Protestant Christian, I've been treated like a kindergartner, and I have begun to suspect that ministers often believe we can't handle the full story, we wouldn't be able to understand, or it would overly complicate the message. Either that or, God forbid, the ministers themselves don't know the full story.

Take, for instance, the purification of the temple story, the one in which Jesus makes a whip and drives out the money changers and the merchants who are selling livestock. Here's the way I've always understood this story: Jesus got angry and drove those folks out of the temple because their presence was defiling the temple. Okay. Way to go, Jesus!

But I never learned why those businesspeople were there in the first place. Here's the answer: The money changers were there because people coming to worship from all over the countryside brought different kinds of money. There was no real standard. Here's the catch: the temple authorities would accept as offerings only a certain kind of currency. Thus, the moneychangers were performing an important service for the worshipers and were, in fact, facilitating certain aspects of worship.

Okay, what about the livestock? They had a similar purpose. Worshipers were to make sacrifices of animals (goats, birds, etc., depending on the worshipers' means). It would have been, for many of them, a hardship to transport livestock from their homes to the temple. Thus, the livestock merchants were performing an important supporting role in worship.

Jesus was a devout Jew, and presumably he knew about the important role of those he threw out of the temple. So what made him so angry?

From my reading, it seems that the money changers and livestock merchants had set up shop in the only part of the temple where poor people and women were allowed to worship. Thus, such was Jesus' regard for those who are left out, that presumably he lost his temper and made a place for them. This strikes me as the real story because Jesus preached on behalf of the poor and the disenfranchised during his entire ministry.

Why didn't anyone ever tell me the whole story? It irritates me that I lived so long as a Christian without this explanation. And it irritates me that I had to find out from my own reading, not from sermons on the episode.

On a more universal level, what has been the result of this widespread understanding of the story? For one thing, this incident was cited as justification in an earlier age for not handling money, for not being a "money changer." Thus, in some European societies the "money changing" was relegated to the Jews, who were then often persecuted and discriminated against partly because they handled the money, a Catch-22 if there ever was one.

Another interpretation I've heard is that this story justifies the use of force or violence because Jesus did it. I've always thought this was a bit of a stretch in trying to enlist God as a supporter of war.

Here's a story told a certain way, with important material left out, that ignores the main point: there must be a place for everyone to worship, and Jesus wants no one left out of the community of faith or given a lesser status in that community. So not only have most of us not been told the whole story, but we've been deprived of a deeper meaning within the story.

Consider now the parable of the Good Samaritan. For years I thought this story was about helping those in need, but that is only part of it.

Here's the setting: Jesus is asked by an expert in the law, "What must I do to inherit eternal life?" Jesus responds by asking, "What is written in the law?" The man then quotes the law about loving God with all you've got and loving your neighbor as yourself. Jesus tells him he is correct in his answers. Then the expert, wanting to test Jesus, asks, "Who is my neighbor?"

That's when Jesus tells the parable of the Good Samaritan.

We all know the story: A man is beaten and left by the road to die. Along come the big-time religious guys, and they pass him by. They can't be bothered to help. Finally, a Samaritan comes along, helps the man, takes him to an inn, pays his bills, and so on. Moral: The Samaritan was the only true neighbor to the suffering man.

But there's more to it. Remember that Jesus is talking to an expert in the Jewish law about who his neighbor is. In doing so, Jesus chose a main character who would be the antithesis of a "neighbor" to this legal expert and to anyone else who happened to be listening. In fact, in the opinion of Jesus' listeners, a "good Samaritan" was an oxymoron. A Samaritan was someone with whom these listeners would never associate. It would be like telling a group of Americans in our time a story about the "good radical Islamist" and expecting them to love that neighbor as themselves.

This makes the parable stronger and much in keeping with Jesus' admonition to love our enemies, to be kind to those who persecute us, and so on.

But wait, this is not the whole story either. Why wouldn't those fine holy men stop and help the injured man? Was it because they were bad, insensitive, uncaring people? No, it was because these men were not ordinary Israelites. They were, respectively, a Priest and a Levite. Thus, under the purity code, the part of the law by which they lived their lives, they would be ritually defiled by touching a corpse. With someone seriously injured, you never know when a person might die, perhaps even while you were touching that person. Then you would have violated the code, the law.

Jesus was saying that when the rules, the code, the law get in the way of mercy and love of one's fellow man, then we need to reexamine those rules.

Why am I making such a big deal of this? It's not only that I'm a bit resentful of having been treated like a child all these years, it's that the real importance of these stories for Christians in the world today is not on the surface; it is in the historical context and the story underneath the surface.

My late brother used to say biblical scholarship is a form of worship, and I believe that's true. Thus I know that some theologians and Bible scholars may have interpretations that differ from what I've written here. Good. I wish I could hear those interpretations as well. The more discussion, the more interpretations, the better.

As a Christian, I want to be treated like a grown-up. I can take it if I hear something that's different from what I've been taught all my life, and I think most other grown-ups can too.

I wrote earlier that I love the Christmas story. But fifteen years ago, I heard a very different and more grown-up version in a Sunday school class. The guest teacher was a friend, a professor of religion, and a good Christian who spent much scholarly effort on the proposition that there was no historical Jesus. Of course, members of the class had trouble understanding how he could be a Christian while also doubting that there even was a historical Jesus, thus there was much discussion as he explained both his theory and his faith.

At one point, an elderly woman asked him, "If there was no historical Jesus, then what does that do to the baby Jesus story and Christmas?"

The professor replied, "You can keep whatever you wish of the Christmas story, but let me tell you what the Christmas story means to me. First, take Mary. She was probably about fourteen years old and pregnant and traveling with a man to whom she was not married.

"Think about it. We know there was no room in the inn, and we've always been led to believe it was because of all the travelers, but I tell you, in that culture at that time, there would have been no room in any inn for an unwed pregnant girl. She was too low down on the social scale to be able to rent a room.

"So there she is, at the bottom of the social ladder, and she has to go have her baby in the barn."

He paused to let the class reflect on what he'd said, then he concluded, "You see, friends, this Christmas story says to me that the lowest-born bastard in the ghetto can rise up and become the spiritual leader of the world. What a wonderful message of hope."

So that's the Christmas story my inner grown-up clings to, even in the midst of the carols, the manger scene, and the beauty of the season.

Barb's Baby

We come to celebrate Christmas
but hear before the service
that a baby was born
with a collapsed lung and crossed arteries,
near death at birth,
and will require one of the new miracles
if he is to come into life
and walk among us,
if he is ever to light the altar candles
or squirm and giggle through a sermon
or play Joseph in the pageant
or sing in the youth choir,
if he is ever to fall in love
with a blond soprano
and try to sit next to her on the bus
on a spring tour to Washington,
if he is ever to leave home someday
and return only for Christmas,
to sit once again with his parents
and celebrate new life
in the place where now we pray
he will simply survive.

Chapter Sixteen

It's Time to Give Those Miracle Stories a Rest

I've advocated for disability rights issues for more than thirty years, and as a Christian I have to say this: Jesus did not make it easy on people with disabilities by performing all those healing miracles. In effect, Jesus was sending a strong anti-disability message, one people with disabilities face every day: "You are not perfect the way you are; something is awry; you don't need an opportunity to be your best self in society; you need to be healed, to be fixed, to be repaired."

Instead of saying, "Take up your bed and walk," what if Jesus had said, "God loves you and I love you just the way you are. Even being unable to walk, you're perfect nonetheless." It may seem a silly comparison, but as the parent of a child with a disability, I prefer Mr. Rogers's message ("I like you just the way you are") to that of Jesus the healer.

At this point I know there are ministers and theologians eager to respond, but I don't want to hear about how those who were healed had "faith that made them whole" or the debates about whether the miracles actually happened or were written later for the early church's agenda. I don't want to hear lectures on the metaphorical value of the miracle stories. Most people are not ministers or theologians; most people either take or reject those biblical miracles at face value.

I believe that Jesus' very embodiment should send a great message, and part of that message is that we, in embodying God, must realize that the most bent, distorted, and disrupted bodies and minds in our midst also embody God.

So my question is, rather than perform the healings, would it not have been an even greater miracle for Jesus to proclaim that those folks—probably thought of as utterly unfortunate, miserable creatures in their society's terms—were as whole and perfect as everyone else?

Imagine it. The friends lower the lame man through the hole in the roof so that Jesus can cure him. Instead, Jesus says something like, "Clearly you are blessed with friends who love you so much they will make this great effort for you to see me. I'm so glad you're here. It gives me the chance to say that God loves you as you are and I love you as you are because you are perfect as you are."

This may sound heretical to those whose ears are attuned to the scriptural version of the story, but as a Christian I believe Jesus really did love the man and really did feel he was perfect the way he was. If Jesus had offered a healing message of love and acceptance and inclusion, those words would have resonated throughout the ages and would have made the lives of millions of people easier. What a miracle *that* would have been!

Consider my son Ronald's confusion about all this. One of the characteristics of autism is the inability to grasp abstractions. Can you think of anything more abstract than God? Try explaining to someone like Ronald about a God who is in here, out there, everywhere but can't be seen or physically touched. Then if you're a Christian, try explaining about Jesus. First there was the virgin birth. What does that mean to someone who doesn't even have a concept of virginity? Then there's the part about Jesus as a man but also as God. As for the concept of the Trinity, I have trouble with that one myself.

Even if you could possibly get a person with autism or another mental disability to grasp these things, you would still have to explain the miracle stories in which Jesus fixes some people with disabilities. And that brings us back to where I started, face to face with the questions about Jesus' regard for a disabled person's value and dignity.

After talking about the miracles, do I then say, "Jesus loves you just the way you are"? If so, how do I answer when Ronald says, "So, Dad, why did he heal the people in the Bible? Didn't he love them just the way *they* were?"

See what I mean? At that point, the miracle stories are not much help. And the idea of a Jesus who heals some people and not others, while professing to love everyone equally, doesn't do a lot for Jesus' credibility either.

So I don't read Ronald the miracle stories. I just try to make him feel that he himself is a miracle, that he is always loved, by his mother and me, his extended family, friends, teachers, and, for whatever it means to him, by God.

At the Autism Conference

A little boy named Nathan
sits on a chair
on a table
elevated so the teachers and parents and grad students
can see him do his tricks.
A man with a foreign accent
and a beard
talks about eye contact
and prompts
and imitative verbalization
and reinforcers,
all the stuff the students are learning to do.
Nathan does what he does
and the students do what they do
and the people clap
and Nathan smiles.

Chapter Seventeen

"Soul Freedom" Under Siege

Several years ago while on a driving trip through a section of the Appalachian Mountains, my wife and I came to a small church. In front of it sat one of those blinking lighted arrows mounted on a small trailer—advertising "Gospel Singing Here Tonight." It had already begun, so we decided to stop.

As we entered the little church, every head turned. We were strangers and we felt strange. The men sat on one side of the church and the women on the other. I realized we'd come into a Primitive Baptist church, or some variation thereof. I became comfortable, yet I could tell that my wife, a Midwestern girl raised in the Disciples of Christ church, was a little uneasy. But the minister shouted, "Welcome. Sit anywhere you like."

We sat together near the back. The service was like many I'd attended as a child and young person in the South, a combination of prayers, congregational singing, and special group performances. After thirty minutes or so, the song leader said, "I'm going to ask our visitors if they have a hymn they'd like us to sing." I asked for "Amazing Grace."

The singing was so much like I'd heard in the little churches of my childhood that I was transported. The voices were raw and reedy but pure and good just like in those churches of yesteryear. I realized how much a part of me that early experience was, and I felt a wave of appreciation that Sally and I had happened upon this service.

We stayed about an hour, and then, after an altar call, more prayers, and more singing, we departed. People stopped the service to wish us safe travels. We were abundantly "God Blessed" and sent on our way.

The memory of this sweet experience brings me to my current dilemma about fundamentalism and how it is understood in society today. I confess that I have something of a love/hate relationship with the evangelical/fundamentalist aspect of contemporary Christianity. First, I don't quite know how to define those terms. I know there are fundamentalists and there are evangelicals and there are evangelical fundamentalists. And I know some evangelicals and some fundamentalists carry on their religious works with quiet dedication, with dignity, and with respect for others. But the ones who don't, and they seem to be in the majority, have created much political mischief in the past twenty-five years.

This is a difficult subject for me because I strongly feel that these folks are undermining some of the basic constitutional rights. Perhaps they don't realize they are undermining the rights that have allowed our country to become one of the most religious in the world, with a wide variety of faiths and ways of worshiping. At the same time, that constitution gives them to right to create their political mischief. And who am I to judge?

Of course, as a young person I didn't even use terms like "evangelical" and "fundamentalist." Mostly, we talked about Baptists, Methodists, Church of Christ people, Pentecostals ("Holy Rollers" we called them), and a few others, plus Catholics.

I had no concept of theology, but I'd ask, "What do the Methodists believe?" I recall my Dad's standard answer: "The Methodists *believe* in backsliding." Then with a smile he'd add, "And the Baptists *do* the backsliding." But questions were generally not encouraged. "All you need to know," we were told, "is that to be saved you have to accept Jesus as your personal savior."

There was also a lot of talk about sin, sinners, and sinning, and that's what is bothering me today. Sin still seems to be the main topic, and in a fact preoccupation, of fundamentalists/evangelicals (combined terms I will use in this essay, admitting as I do so that it does not represent all the people in these categories).

To make myself clear, I have no problem with their faith and how they worship, but I am bothered by their seeming need to define themselves by defining others as sinners. As they have gained political power, they seem intent on making their definitions of sin illegal as well as immoral.

The theologian Marcus Borg writes about old-paradigm Christians and new-paradigm Christians. His definitions and observations appeal to me and I recommend his work to anyone.

Perhaps my view is too-simple-minded, but here's how I've come to think about it: it seems to me that Christianity these days can be viewed as a choice between a rigid, judgmental, exclusive, and punitive Christianity and a loving, abiding, inclusive Christianity.

In the former, the adherents seem preoccupied with other people's sins and see themselves as God's judges and jury on earth. This seems to be the basis for their hostility toward homosexuals, "secular humanists" (their term), civil libertarians, and others.

I'm in the latter group, and while I don't always succeed, I strive to be preoccupied with grace rather than sin and to see myself and others in this group as instruments of God's love on earth. This is the basis for our advocacy for social justice and human rights. We want to affirm our love and support for people regardless of their behaviors as long as those behaviors are not violent and hurtful toward others.

This difference between the two groups is manifest in many areas. It begins, I think, with a basic attitude toward others. In my observation, evangelicals/fundamentalists place a lot of attention on defining themselves by who they are not, and then they seem to need to condemn those "others" for their behavior.

To a scholar of religious studies, I know this seems simple-minded, but it appears to me that evangelicals/fundamentalists often don't have the introspection to examine their attitudes and behavior in this regard. And of course, their judgment of others, especially these days, goes beyond religion and into public policy and politics.

This is a far cry from the fundamentalist churches in which I was brought up. Issues of public policy were not suitable for church talk. My father used to say to me, "Boy, I don't let politics into my pulpit." In that way, he was being true to the Baptist tradition of "soul freedom," the basic belief that co-mingling church and state would be bad for both but probably worse for the church.

While my memories are of the warm community of those churches, it's also true that we concerned ourselves with the scriptural basis for judging certain behaviors as sinful and for deciding whether or not people of other Christian denominations were more sinful than we Baptists.

I thought this way of looking at sin and judging other people was silly then. Now, however, I believe this once-harmless self-righteousness among evangelicals/fundamentalists has been institutionalized and has gone beyond silly to become a threat to the First Amendment's separation of church and state.

Yet, as I write this, I realize I'm doing somewhat the same thing for which I'm criticizing them. I'm judging that they are wrong and I am right. I'm implying that I am among the enlightened Christians and they are stuck in a simplistic worldview.

The problem for me is that I am impelled to speak out on these subjects because—perhaps paternalistically—I feel the evangelicals/fundamentalists are undermining their own future soul freedom by trying to codify sin into the laws and the constitution. In other words, I think they "know not what they do."

But when I said this once in a conversation with a conservative religious radio talk show host, he said, "We know exactly what we're doing."

Where do we Christians go from here? I don't know; I'll say only that we Christians who call ourselves "progressive" probably won't have much influence with Christians who reject our beliefs about how to live a Christian life. My hope is that Jim Wallis and his more moderate evangelicals can provide such a compelling message that the far right evangelicals/fundamentalists will lose their appeal to the great mass of people. Perhaps that will happen, perhaps not. I know this: I am too easily dismissed as a liberal (read "sinner") to have any influence with that segment of our Christian faith. However, I will pray that we work our way through to a respectful and "Christlike" solution.

Television and the Church

Every time I find myself in the little church
where my grandfather and father
preached,
where my uncle led singing conventions
while someone played an upright piano
and pumped an old organ;
every time I feel the air conditioning
and hear the latest hit
from the Top Forty Christian Countdown,
I think,
Damn you, television.

Chapter Eighteen

Sex and the Search for God

Before sex education was taught in school, we learned about it in all kinds of strange ways. When I was about ten years old, my mother carefully explained how babies are made using a metaphor about chickens and eggs.

"The mother has a little nest inside her and there are eggs in the nest," she said. Even at my young age, this stretched belief.

She continued, "Then the father fertilizes the eggs."

Having seen roosters jump on top of hens, I asked, "So did Dad get on top of you to fertilize your eggs?"

"Yes," she said, but added nothing else except, "So that's how babies get to be inside the mother's body and then later become born."

Later my older brother put it in more direct terms.

"You've heard about screwing?" he asked. "That's how you make babies. So you have to be careful if you're going to do it with a girl."

I must have looked confused because he continued, "Did mother tell you all that bullshit about the nest and the eggs?"

Suddenly I realized that screwing was the way eggs were fertilized. My brother confirmed that conclusion, and that was the end of the conversation.

The next day, on the playground in the federal housing project where mother and I lived, I told the guys that I knew how babies were made. When they gathered, I told them it was by screwing. They were astonished. Then a Greek kid named Tommy Bozanis turned red, stuck his finger in his mouth—something he always did when angry—and screamed at me, "My mother would never do that!" Then he punched me in the face with his free hand.

That may have been my first forceful lesson on how difficult it is to talk openly about sex. Of course, in the intervening years, openness about the physical act of sex has increased sometimes beyond what we want to read or view. But there is little openness about the positive spiritual aspects of sexual relations.

The standard Christian belief is that God sent Jesus, the son, into the world embodied as a human to live as a human until the death of his human body, thus it seems logical that the human body itself is a central part of the message. But we don't hear much about it in church.

Somewhere along the way in the development of Christianity, the body/spirit connection seems either to have been lost or considered not important or, worse, condemned as heretical.

The word "God" usually doesn't get connected with sex (although I did hear one "human potential movement" lecturer make the connection by suggesting that the orgasmic cry, "Oh God," is fundamentally a spiritual utterance).

My own religious instruction regarding sexuality and the body boiled down to one word: *Don't!* Don't masturbate. Don't do heavy petting. Don't French kiss. Don't touch beyond holding hands. In the Southern Baptist congregations of my youth, we didn't even talk about sex except when referring to sin, and only then in terms like "fornication" and ."

In dramatic contrast were the pressure-cooker passions of a fundamentalist church service on a hot summer night. On the one hand were the hymns of love and yearning followed by the minister's sermon invoking a heightened state of spiritual awareness or sensitivity, as well as passion; on the other hand were the hot bodies, their sweet and sour smells melding into a musty aroma that, mixed with kerosene and the night air, became the pungent source of everyone's breathing. Out of that intensity people were moved to shout "Amen," to come down the aisle professing their faith in Jesus, to fall into tears with the joy of being born again.

We were inspired into a state of heightened awareness and excitement. It was a transcendent state in which we felt at one with the spirit of God and washed clean of all that went before. I think of it now as having been almost orgasmic in intensity. But that word would not have been allowed into the vocabulary of religious experience.

Yet if sex between two people who love each other can be so much like this revival meeting experience, then why do we learn again and again that the body is dirty, that sex is fornication or adultery, that thinking about our bodies is wrong?

It's time to throw out this way of thinking and speaking, and most particularly within the church. Just because the pop culture has trivialized sex into a cross between entertainment and sport and because the body is often depicted as a center for the ego rather than a center for the spirit does not mean sex and the body are off-limits to God. Sex and spirituality are not opposite ends of the spectrum, and the tendency to think of them that way is neither accurate nor useful to our spiritual growth.

The body is not dirty; sex is not dirty. While it's true that the more progressive or liberal Christian denominations don't speak of the body as dirty, it is also true that, with rare exception, they don't teach about the pleasures of the body as a source of spiritual growth or connection with God. For those of us who believe God is everywhere and in everything, I suggest we should believe that God also resides within the ecstasy of sexual love.

I don't kid myself about the subject of sexuality and spirituality, however. I believe a spiritual connection with another person depends on spiritual intimacy. When appropriate, spiritual intimacy can be enhanced by sexual intimacy, and I believe that in a loving relationship it can even become impossible to separate the two.

Of course, the so-called spiritual quest may camouflage a more base sexual intent, substituting acquisition of the body for aspirations of the soul. We must constantly be willing to examine our true motives in the midst of our passions.

Sexual union should be a powerful manifestation of the divine, an act of co-creation, appreciation for the miracle of life, and a sacred act of communion. We should pay attention to the body, love it, respect it, honor it, and take pleasure in it. Rather than think of the body as a container we live in or as a machine we maintain, we should think of the body as a sacred vessel of the spirit, a reservoir of spirituality, and our most direct physical connection with God. With this appreciation for our own bodies, we would also more easily be able to see the divine in other people.

When my father, a Baptist minister, used to urge people to stop drinking or smoking, he would invoke the Scripture, "Remember the temple to keep it holy," and he would add, "the body is the temple of God."

Dad wouldn't have talked this way about sex, but his quote does bring me to a final thought about sex and the search for God: if the body is indeed the temple of God, then by all means, worship there often with gladness and thanksgiving.

Revival Meeting

How many heavy dusty nights
did I sit on wooden pews beside blonde sweating girls
stirring air toward them with funeral parlor fans
while infants slept finger sucking on quilts
and wasps flew heavy winged from lamp to lamp
searching for a place to fall and burn?

How many booming righteous promises of glory
did I ignore for whispered hints of ecstasy
while nervous deacons sun reddened in overalls
shouted self-conscious amens
and pale children pressed scared faces
into their mothers' laps?

How many stanzas of O Lamb of God I Come
did I sing on key and off
squirming with sweat sticking white shirt and khakis
still fanning and feeling that blonde warmth
while preachers pleaded voice-catching phrases
and babies sucked late-night breasts?

How many big and growing cousins
did I pat on work-hardened backs
standing in the car fume night air
watching them twist hand-rolled bull durhams into their lips
while bats swept wing dodging through the pole light
and blonde girls took sweat-cooling walks?

How many veiled and wrinkled aunts
did I kiss on powdered cheeks
violet bathwater smelling but sour
while blonde girls waited
on the pine needle ground beyond the tombstones
ready with slick and heavy tongue kisses?

And how many mornings have I sat
in the still warm and thick air of the empty church
reading the dim Communion table carvings
while wasps not crisp dead like the others
flew in and out in and out
finding the lamps unlit and the sun too far away?

Chapter Nineteen

Who Would Jesus Kill?

If ever there existed an oxymoron, it is "battle hymn." Yet all my life I've had to listen to "The Battle Hymn of the Republic." As a well-indoctrinated Southern youngster before World War II, I had been taught that "we don't like that hymn," but it was much later before I learned that "we" didn't like it for the wrong reasons.

It turns out I believe the hymn is more than deserving of my condemnation, but not because of anything to do with Southern chauvinism or the Civil War. Rather, it is because the whole idea of soldiers singing a hymn as they march off to kill other soldiers is anathema to me as a Christian.

There's still another reason: the "Republic" should not even have a hymn, either at the time of the Civil War or now. That smacks of civil religion, and if history proves anything, it proves that religion and government do not mix well. Both suffer.

Yet here we are, in the twenty-first century, and some government leaders still invoke Jesus' support and believe they have His approval as we drop bombs, kill people, and maintain the most powerful military machine the world has ever known.

But wait. I'm not talking about foreign policy or military spending; I leave those subjects to others. My cry is only to suggest that we need to get our heads straight about Christianity and the preparing for, and making of, war.

Do we Christians really think Jesus takes sides in a war? When I ask this of fundamentalist friends, they quickly turn to the Jewish Scriptures (what Christians call the Old Testament) to make their case. The Old Testament does contain stories about God helping His people smite their enemies, so it seems that these Scriptures surely justify using violence to do "God's work." Still, it's a bit of a stretch to read those stories about ancient Israel as God's endorsement of war today.

As for the New Testament, I point out to my fundamentalist friends that only in Revelations can we find war talk to any degree, and there's no mention of war in any of the Synoptic Gospels.

I'm aware of St. Augustine's concept of a "just war," though even that rather tortured process strikes me as more a matter of developing a moral rationale than suggesting that God has put a divine seal of approval on war. The other side of that argument, as given by Christian pacifists and others, is that there is never a justification for war.

I do not question that there are moral rationales for war, and though most wars are about power, territory, and access to resources, they surely have also been waged on behalf of compelling moral issues. So yes, I believe there can be a greater moral good served by war, but my Christian faith still does not let me believe there is a "godly" war. I don't believe it. I can't believe it.

And I don't think Christians who feel as I do should let other Christians invoke Jesus as their comrade-in-arms without our challenging it on its face. Jesus said nothing—absolutely nothing—in support of war. Quite the contrary. When (in Luke) his supporters turned to swordplay and cut off the ear of a man among those who came to arrest Jesus, He said, "Enough of this," then healed the ear. He clearly did not want armed violence on His behalf.[1]

Where does Jesus fit into the picture for warriors? I was a jet fighter pilot as a young man. I was prepared to go to war at a moment's notice. I was prepared to drop nuclear bombs, according to my mission plan and in accordance with my belief that, by being ready to do those things, I was helping preserve the peace. I hoped I would never have to do it, but I was trained, prepared, and committed to do it if ordered.

So how do I hold in juxtaposition my Christian faith and the fact that I was prepared to go to war and drop bombs on people?

That was a much easier question to answer when I was younger because I was more inclined to buy into the "righteousness of

American democracy versus the evil of atheistic Communism," as it was so often put in those days. There's a lot of comfort in the cloak of righteousness. But later, in the light of a more mature religious and spiritual worldview, I finally came to this perspective: as a person of faith, I could surely feel a connection with God, feel God's presence with me right there in the cockpit of a machine designed for war, without also feeling that I was doing God's work.

I know now without equivocation that my mission was not a mission on behalf of God but on behalf of humans, and no matter how morally justified I might have felt that mission to be, my reading of Jesus' words precludes ever believing that acts of war can be considered Christian acts.

My final proof of that belief is in the answer to this question: Would Jesus drop the bombs?

---

[1] At this point, my fundamentalist friends will jump on me about at least two scriptural references. In one, Jesus says, "Do not suppose that I have come to bring peace to the earth. I did not come to bring peace but a sword" (Matt 10:34, NIV). Then there is the famous scene in which Jesus makes a whip and throws the merchants and money-changers out of the temple (John 2:14-16, NIV). I'm no biblical scholar, but in the first instance, it seems clear that Jesus is talking not about bringing war but about the inevitable conflict that will arise between what he represents to believers and how the rest of the world will regard his teachings. In the "cleansing of the temple" scene, Jesus obviously was incensed because of the misuse of the temple, and he resorted to violent behavior. I don't read this as a blanket endorsement of violence but will accept that people looking for such an endorsement can find it in this brief Scripture.

On Hearing the Ukrainian Children Sing in Church

Des Moines, Iowa, January 24, 1993

Twenty years before these children were born,
I fought the Cold War
at a small air base in Germany
where I spent the days studying maps,
checking the plan and the bomb,
then practicing,
practicing in my head,
always ready,
even eager
for the call,
and where I spent the nights dressed
in everything but my boots,
waiting for the siren
that would send me running
to be in the air in five minutes,
to use all my skills,
to fly at the speed of sound
to a place I had never been
and had seen only in photographs,
to drop my bomb,
and if I did my job well,
to kill perhaps the parents-to-be
of these very children.

Oh what music the world would have missed.

—from *Life and Work*, 1996

Chapter Twenty

Be Not Afraid

Imam Ako Abdul-Samad, a friend who works with troubled young people, helping them to get off drugs, to get off the street, and to put their lives on a positive track, once told me, "Religion is for people who fear hell; spirituality is for people who've been there." This rang true coming from Ako, who has seen a lot of people who've been there and who has spent a little time in hell himself.

It rang true with me as well, not because I've shared Ako's experiences, but because I first experienced religion as a way to avoid going to hell. The preachers of my childhood were big on illustrating their sermons with stories of dire consequences that befell people who strayed from the narrow path or who had never been on the path.

I listened to tearful sermons of parents who came to Jesus only after the death of a child, or stories of people who survived horrible accidents and in that brush with death saw the power of God and the need to change their lives.

I accept that many people have experienced these kinds of God-revealing episodes, but I can't accept the belief that God visits such tragedy on people to get their attention.

I generally discount the idea of a superparent God up there keeping tally on all the children, but if I did believe in such a deity, I'd still doubt that God deliberately brings harm and grief to people in order to bring them to salvation. Why would God choose to work that way? Even as a young person, I found it confusing that preachers would talk about God's love for us in one breath, then relate how God had taught some unfortunate sinner a cruel lesson. I know the Hebrew Scriptures (what we Christians call the Old Testament) are full of stories of a punishing and vengeful God. Still, I don't believe it. It doesn't make sense.

Put yourself in God's shoes for a minute. If you were the superparent God, would you want people to worship you only after scaring them into it? It seems to me that tactic would produce a good deal of insecurity for God. God might wonder, "Are those folks really sincere, Me-loving, worshipful people, or are they just scared that if they don't go through the motions, I'll smite them tooth and thigh?"

It's hard for me to imagine that kind of divine internal dialogue. I suspect that the fundamentalist preachers' scare tactics are more about how the preachers want God to be rather than how God is.

As for me, I have to conclude that fear never will be a great motivator for religious faith, devotion, and worship. If love doesn't work in connecting people to God, fear doesn't have a chance. After all, the Scripture doesn't say, "God is fear." It says, "God is love."

Ghost Dance

Don't despair the ruined lives,
the crosses to bear,
the churches burned down and smoking,
the rotted blood of hatred,
the civil wars,
crusades,
and inquisitions.
Hey, look who's in your back yard.
It's.........it's Jesus.
He's in everybody's back yard,
everybody's kitchen,
saying, "Look at me.
Get up.
Let's have some coffee.
I'll help you get through this day."
  —James A. Autry, Jr., used by permission.

Chapter Twenty-one

Getting the Government Out of the Church's Business

I'm always amazed as well as perplexed by how concerned some of my fellow Christians are with what other people choose to do with their genitalia. This wouldn't be a big problem if it were simply benign disapproval; instead, their concern has become an obsession with passing laws to criminalize behaviors Christians find sinful.

There's nothing new about this, of course; if anything characterizes "true believers," it is that they feel their calling is not only to obey God's laws as they interpret them, but also to be the enforcers of those laws here on earth. I often feel they are far more preoccupied with humankind's sin than with God's grace.

Recently I found myself in a discussion about gay rights with some of my Southern kinfolks and friends. They stated their objections by citing Scripture. This is to be expected because, in fact, there is no objection whatsoever to gay rights that is not based on religious belief, and it has always struck me that the gay rights discussion inevitably gets stuck in one group's versus another group's interpretation of the Bible. But this misses the point altogether.

"This is not about the Bible," I told my friends and relatives. "It's about the Constitution. Let's suppose I agree with you that homosexuality is a sin. I don't believe it is a sin, but I'm not a biblical scholar and can't quote Scripture to back up my position, so let's just say, for the sake of discussion, that I agree with you that it is a sin. My question is this: 'Are you suggesting that we withhold constitutional liberties from sinners?'"

A giant pause in the conversation followed, because this is the fundamental (no pun intended) question after all.

I continued, "Because if that's what you're suggesting, consider the ramifications. I do remember the Scripture that says, 'We have all sinned and fallen short of the glory of God,' so if we withhold constitutional liberties from people because we judge them to be sinners, then we're all in trouble, aren't we? None of us will have constitutional liberties, right?"

As with most of these conversations, my folks just got angry. "This is different," they said.

"So let me get this straight," I replied. "You want to withhold constitutional liberties from some sinners, just the ones you judge to be the most sinful of the sinners. Is that right?"

The conversation should have ended, but they then launched into their old saw about how gays don't want equal rights, but they want special rights. I'd heard all that before when I was a kid growing up in Tennessee and Mississippi, only in those days it was said about African Americans. Then in the seventies, I heard it about women.

I believe the issue of gay rights is the most intense church/state issue facing the country today, and yet it rarely gets framed in that way. Clearly there may be "sinful" behaviors that should also be illegal (murder and theft come to mind), but to pass laws selectively in support of our religious beliefs about other people's behavior is to make us vulnerable to any number of encroachments on the wall of church/state separation.

Which brings me to the hot potato of gay marriage. Again, relying on the concept of the separation of church and state, I believe we need to separate the two aspects of marriage, one of which is the business of the state and one of which is the business of the church.

One of those aspects is the contract of marriage; the other is the covenant of marriage. Clearly the contract part—property rights, tax issues, inheritance rights, hospital visitation rights, and so on—is an appropriate concern of the state. But the covenant part—love; commitment; emotional, psychological, and spiritual bonds and support—is not an appropriate concern of the state. Thus, I believe we should separate the two aspects and call the contract part a civil union and call the covenant part a "marriage." The state can legitimately continue to issue licenses for civil unions, but let the churches address "marriage" as a sacrament of the church and in accordance with the churches' own policies.

As our churches, even many of the more progressive congregations, struggle with their own issues of gay rights within the community of faith, they should assert, loud and clear, that even if they themselves withhold certain rights and privileges and even sacraments from gay men and lesbians, the state should stay out of it.

The Edge of Love

I lived too long on the edge of love,
making romance into love, making sex into love,
thinking I could discover the circumstances
in which love would reveal itself
like some Shangri-la
appearing out of the mists
after an arduous and desperate search.

But love waited for the inevitable,
showing itself at last in the unexpected terrain of loss,
waiting until grief exposed the unguarded me
to something I could not get or have or do,
could not see or hold, until I understood
that love is first about the possibilities of life
then about the certainty of loss
and finally about the exquisite pain of both.

Chapter Twenty-two

Just How Truly Accommodating Are Churches?

It is a tradition in my church, as in many others, for a different family to light an Advent candle on each of the Sundays leading up to Christmas. I was surprised and moved a couple of years ago when a gay couple lit the candle one Sunday. I should not have been surprised, because our church is an "open and affirming" congregation, meaning we affirm committed homosexual relationships and profess to open our membership and full participation in the church to all people.

Still, I found myself becoming emotional at the presence of this couple because it represented to me such an important statement. After all, if we can't imbue worship with equality and justice as well as fellowship, how will we ever be able to bring those qualities to the larger society?

But my pride was diminished somewhat that Sunday when, after the service, I noticed that the Advent candles were elevated in a place that could not be approached by wheelchair. How in the world, I wondered, could a church so sensitive to the needs of people, particularly those who have been discriminated against, put the Advent candles in a location unreachable from a wheelchair?

The answer, I fear, is that people with disabilities are often *in* the church but are not so often *of* the church. They are welcomed, they are treated with courtesy and respect, but they are not fully honored in that they are considered people to be served and not people who have service to contribute. If we believe God is within us, then we must believe that the most bent, distorted, and disrupted bodies and minds in our midst also embody God and that they have much to give and much to teach us.

I have talked with friends in other churches and find the same situation. Churches will often say they are loving and accepting and supportive of people with disabilities, but that attitude boils down to building a ramp for a wheelchair or providing amplified listening devices. I know many churches work hard to demonstrate God's love, and I believe they are sincere in those efforts, but it is not enough simply to make it easier for people with disabilities to get up the steps and through the door.

Our attitudes have been influenced, to be sure, by the stories of Jesus' healing miracles, but the deeper question of those stories has to do with the healing that we as Christians should be bringing to the world. If we are serious about this mission, there's no better place to begin than with the disabled people right in our midst, and often right in our churches.

A few questions for consideration by congregations of any faith:

• Just how accessible are the churches? Why weren't the churches the first to make their buildings accessible to the disabled? Why did some of them exempt themselves from what every other public building was required to do? Many still are not wheelchair accessible. I've attended some of these churches and have been impressed by the people who stand by to physically pick up the wheelchairs and help disabled individuals into the church. Surely that is an act of love. But it can also be felt by the disabled people to be another sign that they remain the dependent outsiders, the *others*, even here at church.
• Beyond simple physical accommodation, why aren't more people with disabilities involved in the governance of churches, serving on the councils, the boards of deacons, and so on?
• What about participation in the worship service itself? Most people in wheelchairs would be able to pass the collection plate or serve Communion and be involved in other active ways.
• How many congregations invite mentally disabled people to participate in worship and become active members of the community of

faith? Given a chance, most mentally disabled people can greet congregants, hand out literature, show people to a seat, or collect the offering. Could not the richness of this experience—for everyone—more than offset whatever small glitches might occur?

• How many churches actively seek to establish group homes and other supported environments in their neighborhoods? The negative side of that question is, how many churches and/or their members have worked to keep such places *out* of their neighborhoods?

• From a parent's viewpoint, why are there not more religious education programs adapted specifically for kids with mental disabilities? The public schools adapt the curriculum for these young people; why can't the churches?

• How many churches sponsor support groups for parents, siblings, or friends of people with disabilities?

I know some churches can give positive answers to all my questions, but they are in the minority. Frankly, I haven't even found many ministers or lay leaders who are comfortable with these questions. It's as if they think I'm being provocative by asking, rather than truly seeking answers or offering suggestions.

But I do so because I have a rather intractable viewpoint. With all that people with disabilities face in this world—the stares, the social exclusion, the lack of employment opportunities, the lack of parity in insurance coverage for mental illness, the cost of their special health needs, and the maddeningly patronizing attitudes of even well-meaning people—they should be able to depend on their churches for unconditional love and support, for complete acceptance, for recognition and appreciation of their talents, and for the same full and rich spiritual experience available to every member of their community of faith.

Leo

He threw water on my motorcycle's one sparkplug
so I wouldn't be able to leave him,

so I would have to stay
his buddy
and play in the backyard,
the only place he was allowed to go.

Early before anyone was up
he would fill a tumbler with tap water
then sneak out the front door
of his side of the duplex
and tiptoe to where the Harley 125 was chained
and pour a little puddle around the plug.

Later, late and frustrated,
drying the plug, grease on my hands,
I would yell at him
"Goddammit, Leo, you're making me late,
I've got to go to school,"
and sometimes chase him and pretend
I was going to hit him.
But he would only repeat what he said
every morning of every day of every year
we lived in that duplex:
"You Leo's buddy
Play with Leo now."

Leo would stand,
his big droopy frame shutting out the light
from the back screen door,
and watch mother cook.
"Rufe play with Leo?"
His breathing was noisy
and he sometimes drooled
and his eyes looked in different directions.
Mother would say "That big dumb thing
scares me and I wish they'd keep him
off the back porch,"

and I would say "If he's so dumb
how does he know to ground out my sparkplug?"

We knew his age and his mind's age
and we knew they didn't match,
but we didn't know anything else
except he was Italian
and his big family kept him there with them,
in the duplex,
and they had barbecues in the backyard
and drank beer and laughed with each other,
and that Leo played on the ground
with the other children
like a big pet, I thought.
And they all seemed happy enough.

I hadn't thought about Leo in years, of course,
until just the other day,
just after the tests were in,
just after the pediatrician
in his I am your friend voice
said something to us like,
"Well, he'll never go to Harvard Medical School,
but he'll be very functional
and will be able to do a lot of things."

Later, I wondered if that meant things like
ground out a sparkplug with a glass of water
or play the family pet
with children a third his age.
And I thought,
sometimes God makes you write things on the blackboard
a thousand times.

    —from *Life After Mississippi*, 1989

Chapter Twenty-three

Sex and Sunday School

Our society has a paradoxical relationship with the subject of sex. On the one hand we pay way too much attention to sex; on the other we pay way too little attention to sex. We make it both too important and not important enough.

I've found these same attitudes in church. In my youth there were a lot of "thou shalt nots" about doing sex, but no "thou shalts" for learning about sex. Some churches now engage the subject directly with children and teenagers, but more often than not the lessons are still about morality-based prohibitions. In fact, "abstinence education" has become all the rage among conservative politicians as well as conservative Christians.

I don't refute abstinence as a choice, but given the pervasiveness of sex in the pop culture, along with normal hormonal development, I submit that abstinence is not likely to become all the rage among teenagers.

Yet there are moral issues beyond "doing it" or "not doing it" that humans of any age should consider, and I think the church should take a role in presenting those issues as well as whatever position the church wants to take on abstinence.

In fact, I feel so strongly about sex as a powerful manifestation of the divine in human life that I think churches should offer sex education that transcends the mechanical and physical, as it is taught in schools, and concentrates instead on the spiritual. We need to recognize that kids *are* going to think about sex and talk about sex, and any adult can predict how they're going to think about it and what they're going to say.

So I suggest that church teachers need to give our young people other ways to think and talk about the subject. I think we need to challenge kids to develop a broad moral sensibility and appreciation for aspects of sexuality not taught in school or through the pop media. And where better for this kind of education than at home and church?

Here are some approaches religious teachers might consider:

- *Sex as co-creation.* Reproductive mechanics are one thing—leave that to the parents and schools—but creating a human being is quite another. It is in the process of having a baby, more than any other of our experiences, that we are given a role in the great mystery of life, that we become makers of a miracle, co-creators—with one another and with God—of life itself. What a powerful concept for young people to learn. I do not believe this would encourage them to rush into parenthood but instead would help imbue them with a sense of awe about the process of birth and would increase their sense of responsibility about their roles in it.

- *Sex as appreciation of the body.* Our own bodies are miracles in themselves, yet we try to reduce that mystery to a series of superficial sensual experiences. Popular culture creates body images based only on appearance, thus young people are led to believe that only certain bodies—usually those that look quite different from their own—are desirable. Religious sex education should teach appreciation for the physical body as part of the miracle of life and include ways we should love our bodies and take care of them, from diet and exercise to sheer sensual and erotic appreciation of how we look and feel.

- *Sex as sacred and spiritual.* Sex can be one of life's most sacred acts and one of its most unique spiritual treasures. While our pop culture seems to regard it as an athletic event, sex is deepest and most pleasurable as an act of meditation or even prayer. Church leaders could teach how people of other faiths consider and practice sex as a contemplative or sacred relationship. Also, it should be emphasized to young people that when they begin to have sex, they should strive to move beyond the physical and to embrace sex with the spirit as well as the body so that they can experience what I think God intended—a divine wholeness not only with the partner but with life itself. Teaching this attitude, I believe, will help students put the right, as well as the right amount of, emphasis on sex.

- *Sex as communion.* There should be no denial of the physical pleasure and titillation of sex, but we should also teach that its most meaningful and fundamental purposes are more about communion than self-gratification. Through sex, we can be attentive to the other, we can serve the other, we can rejoice in the other, we can bless and be blessed with the other.

- *Sex as a moral act.* Even when the intent has nothing to do with the spiritual, sex should be mutual and it should be honest. It is said that women trade sex for love and men trade love for sex. It's time to straighten out that equation, change it from a trade to an agreement, and make it honestly about sex or about love or, ideally, about both. Neither love nor sex should be trivialized as a commodity to be traded.

  As for birth control, it is less about mechanics than about integrity, respect, and responsibility. The moral goals of birth control are concerned with love and not fear, and they go far beyond the immediate concerns of unwanted pregnancy.

- *Sex as celebration.* Let us teach our kids that, while sex should be taken seriously, it should also be embraced with thanksgiving as a joyful, extravagant celebration of life, of communion, of the body itself, and of the connection with God.

Living with the Body

There are no rules for making peace with the body.
It's always trial and error, give and take,
on-the-job training.

This is not about diet and exercise,
this is about how hard it is
to make the body welcome in your life
instead of ignoring it
like an embarrassing relative in the back room.

For sixty years I have remembered the day
Mother jerked my face from her lap
because she felt the heat of my breath,
signaling to both of us,
I suppose,
that I could no longer be her baby boy.

Consider now the dilemma of Ronald
who struggled so hard to find his body in space,
learning finally to walk without falling,
who despite all the life science classes
and my straightforward explanations
still is confused and amused and sometimes alarmed
by his own erections.
What could be so concrete and yet so abstract?
And how could such a thing be explained
to a mind without even an understanding
of the age-old mechanics of the body
much less a way to imagine
the love, joy, and exhilaration of a union
that transcends the merely physical?

Then again, that's where we all struggle,
learning how to live peacefully within the body,
making it so welcome, so familiar, so intimate
that we no longer can tell
where the physical ends and the spiritual begins.

Chapter Twenty-four

The Trouble with Prayer

Assuming we Americans are waiting, as we always seem to be, for the last word and the final proof, *USA Today* has reported a six-year study showing that people who pray or meditate live longer than those who don't. Not only that, but other studies reported in the same article suggest a large variety of health benefits resulting from prayer.

So what do we do now, add it to our endless list of healthy practices? In addition to the echinacea, vitamins C and E, gingko biloba, folic acid, beta carotine, saw palmetto, and an aspirin a day, I'll now also say a prayer. That should do it. One bothersome question, though: if I were to decide to add prayer to the daily health regimen, doesn't that reduce God to kind of a health maintenance consultant?

I'm kidding, of course, yet I did have a fleeting moment of wondering just what, as a person who prays, I am supposed to do with the information about the health benefits of prayer.

Prayer is already the most perplexing of spiritual activities for me. I think this is due to some kind of fundamental conflict I feel. On the one hand, I read about and want to embrace one or another ways of thinking about and participating in prayer. I want to be meditative, I want to breathe prayer instead of saying it, I want to concentrate on gratitude for all life's blessings instead of asking for something else. I want to feel prayer in my everyday relationships with my wife, my children, my friends, even my home and garden. In other words, I want a prayer life, if that's what I should call it, that does not begin or end with words. No "Gracious God" or" Heavenly Creator," no "I ask it in the name of Jesus" or even any "amens."

And yet I read about the various categories of prayer such as intercessional prayer, devotional prayer, confessional prayer, centering prayer, and so on, and while I seem to have an almost organic distaste for categorizing anything of the spirit, there are times I find myself saying one of these prayers. There are times I need to be specific, to express my fears, to ask for something special, something beyond the everyday blessings of a rich and fulfilling life. Yes, there are even times when I want a miracle.

Right now, I want my beloved sister-in-law Susie to be healed from her pancreatic cancer. Twenty-two years ago, I wanted her late husband, my brother, to be healed from his bone marrow cancer. I prayed mightily for his healing, and I'm doing the same now for Susie. And when people tell me they will remember her in their prayers, I am profoundly grateful for that.

After my brother's death, I wrote the following poem:

Against All Those Desperate Prayers

Against all those desperate prayers
whispered in airplanes
and hospital corridors
Against all those deals and bargains
of new beginnings and new behaviors I thought God
could not afford to pass up
Against all the wild promises
he died anyway.

I still pray that my son with autism might somehow come out of his disability and live a more normal life, be able to live independently, hold a job, and have a love relationship.

I pray that my wife may have the health and strength to carry out what she has chosen to do in public service. I pray that my children and grandchildren will be protected and healthy and happy.

So the conflict seems to be between some deeper understanding or relationship I want to have about and with prayer, one that transcends words themselves—what I call the "Thank you, God" prayers—versus what I think of as a more naive, childlike relationship with prayer—the ones I call the "Gimmie, God" prayers.

Notice I'm not talking about a relationship with God here, though certainly prayer is part of that relationship. I'm talking about how to get myself straight about prayer, how to hold to my need for a transcendent experience that words would only trivialize while not letting go of (and not judging harshly) my child's need to give God my wish list of blessings every once in a while.

Lord knows, it's a dilemma.

Learning to Pray

Ronald has heard people pray,
the ministers at church,
his grandfather at family gatherings,
me at the dinner table,
and he knows there's supposed to be something important
about those words and phrases,
but he doesn't get them right,
the prayers;
of course, he doesn't get a lot of things right.
"Grateful God," he says,
"Thank you for my ceiling fan
and my lawn mower and my cat . . ."

Once for no reason I could discern,
he stopped cutting the grass,
letting the mower engine die,
raised hands to face and said,
"You are a grateful God for giving me this Lawn Boy."
And in the Lord's Prayer he says,
"Hallowed be my name."

I used to think I should teach him to pray
the way everyone else does

but lately I don't know,
lately I find myself asking,
"How do I know that God is not
also to be grateful?"
Lately, I think less about God's majesty
and more about Ronald's struggle
to make sense of his place in this world,
never mind the next world.

Lately, I hear myself praying,
"Grateful God safely tucked away in Heaven,
we are thankful that Ronald
(hallowed be his name)
has come to live among us
in order that we may learn
how to face our disabilities,
how to find joy in ceiling fans and lawn mowers,
and how to pray."

Chapter Twenty-five

I Love Jesus the Man

Some years ago after I walked down the aisle to change my membership to a Disciples of Christ Church, the minister, as was the custom, took my hand and asked among other things, "Do you affirm that you believe Jesus is the son of the living God?" I responded, as William Blake did when asked a similar question, "Yes," then quietly added, "And so am I and so are you."

The minister's eyes widened but he smiled.

Was I just being a smart aleck or trying to establish myself as an iconoclast? No, but I was wanting to express my discomfort with all the ritualistic questions and answers we engage in at church.

I know that, as a Christian, I am supposed to accept unquestioningly the divinity of Jesus, and I do—but I also believe the divinity resides in all of us. When I make this point, however, the next question from a fellow Christian is usually "Do you believe Jesus is God?" And that's where my trouble begins.

It's not that I don't believe Jesus is God, it's that I'm not concerned about it one way or another. It is my understanding that there is much scholarly debate on this point. Some scholars point out that the Gospel of John is the only one that explicitly makes the claim that Jesus is God; other scholars disagree.

I understand also that, within this debate, there is the question of when Jesus became divine. Most say, "at birth, of course." Others say, "After John the Baptist baptized him and the heavens opened up and God announced that Jesus was his son in whom he was well pleased."

At the risk of sounding utterly sacrilegious, this is the point at which I say that it doesn't concern me very much. My Christian faith doesn't turn on that question, and how I try to live my faith is much more focused on Jesus the human rather than Jesus the God.

We Christians are always professing that we want to be "Christ-like" in our lives. Yet in a way, Jesus as God gives us an out, a readymade excuse when we fall short. After all, Jesus was divine, perfect, right? Thus how can we mere mortals be expected to be Christlike? How can we be expected to live a life of goodness and compassion every day? It's not "human."

But in my view, this presents the great Christian challenge. If we think of Jesus as human, as a man rather than God, it takes away the "God" excuse. And in a way, it liberates us to examine our place in the world, our relationship to the human condition, and our role in healing whatever we can in this world.

I love the man that Jesus was. I love the way he treated his friends, how he shared his wisdom with everyone who would listen, how he always stuck up for the poor, the disabled, the children, the weak, and the disenfranchised. He embodied goodness and compassion and in doing so showed us how to embody the love that can reveal the divine in us, even as it did in him.

I don't talk about this subject much because it seems to make some other Christians indignant. One even said to me, "If it doesn't matter to you that Jesus was divine, then you can't call yourself a Christian."

Oh yes I can. And I do.

My Five Top Theological Questions

In the previous essay, I tried to address my concerns about concentrating so much on the divinity of Jesus. I want to add what I call my top five theological questions.

1. How could God be loving, generous, and merciful, and then arrange for his own son to be tortured and killed? Is this to suggest that this was God's only—or even best—option for bringing salvation to the world? The atonement theology has never made much sense to me.

2. If it's true that we believers have all been washed clean of our sins by the blood sacrifice of Jesus, why are many churches so intent on pointing out our sins, some even going so far as to classify and diagram sin according to type and severity?

3. If God forgives us and loves us regardless of our foibles and mistakes, regardless of what we do, then why should there be such admonition for us to love God in return? Does it make a difference to God? Doesn't this imply that God won't forgive us after all if we aren't professing our love for God?

4. Isn't the concept of the Holy Trinity kind of a dodge, to allow us Christians to be polytheistic while claiming to be monotheistic? I understand the division—Creator, Redeemer, and Sustainer—but what difference does it make? I know we talk about the three in one, but why talk about the three at all? If we need these concepts, wouldn't it be better, and simpler, to talk about the three aspects of God? Which of course begs the question of how come there are only three?

5. Why is the virgin birth so important? In fact, why is it important at all? Would Jesus be any less perfect, any less a man, any less a God, any less a role model if his mother were not a virgin? And if so, what does *that* say about the possibilities for the rest of us? Would Mary be less blessed, less worthy, or less a mother? Or is the real question *would she be too much of a woman?* And if so, what does that say about women, not to mention sexuality?

Just asking.

Recommended Reading

I do not intend the following list to serve as a bibliography for this book; rather, it is simply a partial list of books I've read over the years that have meant a lot to me and that, to one degree or another, bear on my writing. There is not one particular viewpoint that emerges from these writings; indeed, you will find many viewpoints. I commend them all for your consideration.

A Cry of Absence, Martin Marty
A Passion for the Possible, William Sloane Coffin
A World Waiting to Be Born, M. Scott Peck
Beyond Belief, Elaine Pagels
Chop Wood, Carry Water, Rick Fields with Peggy Taylor, Rex Weyler, and Rick Ingrasci
Embodiment, James Nelson
How Can I Help? Ram Dass and Paul Gorman
Hymn to an Unknown God, Sam Keen
I and Thou, Martin Buber
Into the Whirlwind, John Shelby Spong
Life and Holiness, Thomas Merton
Living Buddha, Living Christ, Thich Nhat Hanh
Man's Search for Meaning, Viktor Frankl
On Caring, Milton Mayeroff
Original Blessing, Matthew Fox
Shambala, The Sacred Path Of The Warrior, Chogyam Trungpa
Studies in Mystical Religion, Rufus Jones
Tao Te Ching, Lau Tzu, translation by Stephen Mitchell
The Chalice and the Blade, Riane Eisler
The Courage to Be, Paul Tillich
The Gnostic Gospels, Elaine Pagels
The Gospel According to Jesus, Stephen Mitchell
The Intimate Connection, James Nelson
The Only Necessary Thing, Henri J. M. Nouwen
The Road Less Traveled, M. Scott Peck

The Sacred Journey, Frederick Buechner
The Secret Life of the Soul, J. Keith Miller
The Student Bible, New International Version
To a Dancing God, Sam Keen
To Love and Be Loved, Sam Keen
Touching Peace, Thich Nhat Hanh
Why Christianity Must Change Or Die, John Shelby Spong
Wishful Thinking, A Theological ABC, Frederick Buechner

Note: There is far too much poetry to recommend, but if you are not already a reader of sacred and/or mystical poetry, I suggest you begin with an anthology: *The Enlightened Heart,* compiled and edited by Stephen Mitchell.